The Free Church

The Free Church

Franklin Hamlin Littell

STARR KING PRESS
Beacon Hill Boston

Library of Congress catalog card number: 57-10927

Printed in the United States of America

Franklin Hamlin Littell is director of Franz Lieber Haus, an American educational institution in Germany. A graduate of Cornell College (Iowa), he received a B.D. degree from the Union Theological Seminary in 1940 and a Ph.D. degree from Yale in 1946. From 1949 to 1951 he served as a member of the religious affairs staff of the United States High Commissioner for Germany. From 1951 to 1953 Dr. Littell was dean of the chapel of Boston University. He returned to Germany in 1953 to become senior representative of the Franz Lieber Foundation, St. Paul, Minnesota. Dr. Littell is also chairman of the Ecumenical Committee of the German Kirchentag (Laymen's Movement). He is author of *The Anabaptist View of the Church: An Introduction to Sectarian Protestantism,* which has received the Brewer award of the American Society of Church History and is to be published in a revised edition by the Starr King Press.

In Memory of

David E. Roberts

Teacher and Friend

Preface

The invitation of the directors of the Menno Simons Foundation to give the annual Menno Simons Lectures was extended three times to out-groupers before Professor Robert J. Kreider, himself a Mennonite, came to the speaker's platform. That the first invitations were extended to members of sister Free Churches is a tribute to the generosity of spirit for which the Mennonites are well known; it also reveals the extent to which study of the Anabaptist/Mennonite heritage has become a common concern of the children of the "Left Wing of the Reformation" — the largest percentage of which bear other names than "Mennonite." Interest in Anabaptist/Mennonite studies not only has produced in the last three decades a remarkable renaissance of scholarship within the Mennonite fold, but is drawing together a growing number of scholars in other communions, both in Europe and America. This is a new development in the four hundred and twenty-five years of Free Church history, and an encouraging one.

When the great Heidelberg church historian, Professor Walther Koehler, one of the first outsiders to catch a glimpse of the uniqueness of this tradition, was asked to write on "Anabaptism" for the second edition of *Die Religion in Geschichte und Gegenwart,*[1] he centered his statement in the proposition:

> The Anabaptists are the Bible Christians of Reformation history, distinguished from the Reformers through the extension of the Biblical norm beyond the purely religious into economic and social life.

When Harry Emerson Fosdick published his *Great Voices of the Reformation* a short time ago he considered it fitting to reserve forty pages for Anabaptist/Mennonite documents.[2] Quite evidently a major change of attitude has occurred in recent years. Students who have referred to the primary sources are beginning to see that the traditional hostility to the pioneer Free Churchmen was more political and ecclesiastical than anything else. As persons of democratic conviction become more certain that coercion in matters of religious faith is both immoral and ultimately self-defeating, a kindlier assessment of the Anabaptist/Mennonite testimony by outsiders is inevitable. There are still historians, and indeed church historians, who are ignorant of the actual facts about Anabaptist history and teaching but, as such an excellent manual as Dillenberger and Welch's *Protestant Christianity* makes plain, the tide is changing.[3]

Most significant, perhaps, is the collaboration of non-Mennonites in the growing series of primary sources on Anabaptism published under the auspices of the Verein fuer Reformationsgeschichte. Friendly outsiders there have always been, from Gottfried Arnold (1666-1714) to Henry C. Vedder (1853-1935) ; what has been most needed is to let the movement speak for itself. That primary sources are now available to the serious student of the origins of the Free Church is real cause for rejoicing. Moreover, as one looks back over the generations which were shamed by discrimination and often bloodied by persecution, one can only give thanks for a change of spirit between the churches. A fitting symbol of this was the participation of Professors Oskar Farner and Fritz Blanke of the University of Zurich in special exercises at the Fifth Mennonite World Conference (Basel, 1952), during which a service was held where Manz was drowned and a memorial plaque was set on the Grebel House.[4] Manz and Grebel were once damned as heretics by the standing order. Such a representative rectification of old wrongs is a sign that the churches have learned something in the School of Christ over the generations. It is also clearly implied that the early leaders of the Swiss Brethren were not accidentally or criminally at odds with the authorities, but rather sealed with their blood a Christian testimony no longer to be regarded as marginal but rather worthy of being judged on its own merits. The Free Church testimony has not only endured but strengthened through the years.

Increased interest in Anabaptist/Mennonite studies is

quite evidently not limited to historical and philological pursuits, but affects the life of the Church itself. The doctrine of the Church, the role of the laity, the doctrine of the Holy Spirit, the various articulations of Christian ethical concern — all are affected by the adequacy or inadequacy of our understanding of what the pioneers of the Free Church were about. The renaissance of intellectual discipline and scholarly effort among the Mennonites, one of the most striking phenomena in American Protestantism today, can have the most salutary effect on the future of the faith as held by other denominations as well. The American denominations as a whole are still suffering to a marked degree from the effects of nineteenth-century liberalism; their theological and ethical "tone" (or lack of it) is strongly reminiscent of the "culture religion" of Great Britain in the Victorian era and Imperial Germany before World War I. The appalling chasm between Christ and culture, a fact of the Christian life which most of our European brethren have painfully rediscovered in the twentieth century, is not yet obvious to large sections of American religious thought and life. The difficulty of discourse between persons still safely lodged in an intact society and those across the sea who have again become, literally or figuratively, pilgrims in search of a city with foundations, has become one of the basic impediments to the trans-Atlantic dialogue.

There are those American Christians, to be sure, who have preserved — albeit in somewhat crystallized and sterilized form — the outlines of classical Christian belief. Professor Otto H. Piper of Princeton commented a few years ago on the matter as follows:

> Notwithstanding the obvious weaknesses of fundamentalism it is deeply to be regretted that up to the present moment it is hardly represented at all in the ecumenical movement. Its numerical strength especially in the United States is so considerable and the spiritual influence of its leaders reaches such wide circles that as a result of their absence the ecumenical Church obtains a completely distorted view of American Protestantism.

> Furthermore their non-participation gives a dangerous impetus to subjectivism in a country whose theologians have previously embraced so enthusiastically and often unintelligently the liberalism of nineteenth century European theology.[5]

But fundamentalism can be as puerile as liberalism can be vapid; neither does justice to the Gospel, and the most significant theological and scholarly developments in contemporary Christian thought are post-fundamentalist and post-liberal.

"Fundamentalism" is, in any case, an inappropriate term for the classical Anabaptist/Mennonite testimony, as inappropriate as "pietism." "Orthodoxy" will not serve, for usage has limited it to doctrinal issues. "Integral" Christianity, which presumes faithfulness in both intellectual and ethical areas, is perhaps as good a term as any. But however termed, the Mennonite form of the faith in America, which has learned the values of the comparative historical method without swallowing the poisons of contemporary gnosticism, has much to contribute to American Protestantism as a whole. Much of the American Mennonitism has, to be sure, been corrupted by individualism (pietism, the Enlightenment) and fundamentalism (revivalism); but a Methodist may feel free to comment that the best Mennonite leaders display that quality of intellectual precision and spiritual earnestness which is needed in all Protestantism today, and to wish that the same were true of his own large and prosperous denomination.

Nowhere is the Anabaptist/Mennonite testimony more valuable than in its clear statement and open witness as to the nature of the Church itself. For the essence of Anabaptist concern was the nature of discipleship, conceived in terms of Christian community; in short, in the view of the Church.[6] In many confessions today the role of the laity is still disputed; the Mennonites have always been clear that the Church is the People of God, and the People is the Church. Not long ago the writer received a letter from a professor of theology in one of Germany's great theological faculties, in which was said:

> In the past Semester I had for the first time a four hour major course on "The History of the Christian Mission from the Reformation to the Present," and discovered my previous impression to be justified, that the whole misery of German Protestantism is rooted in the fact that from the very beginning the Reformation (churches) became nothing but pastor-churches. The same church which discovered the priesthood of all believers has up to the present day never understood how to develop a real sense of responsibility in the Christian laity, with spontaneous cooperators in the local churches.[7]

The laymen are frequently active in the American churches, but the theological problem remains widespread. In the words of a son of the Mennonite fold who is now a brilliant leader in the Protestant Episcopal Church, ". . . the doctrine of the Church, with the related doctrine of the Holy Spirit, are the forgotten doctrines of Christian tradition."[8] An understanding of the Anabaptist/Mennonite tradition is basic to Christian reform today. A studied referral to the classical testimonies of the Free Church movement can be illuminating both for the Church and for the political society at large.

To President-Emeritus Ed. G. Kaufmann, President D. C. Wedel, and Professor Cornelius Krahn of Bethel College (North Newton, Kansas), who extended a fraternal invitation in connection with the Menno Simons Lecture Series (1954) and lent brotherly assistance and encouragement to the publication of the lectures as revised, the writer is deeply indebted. He is, of course, responsible for their final form.

F. H. L.

Bad Godesberg/Rhein

Contents

The Free Church

I. The Basic Issues, the Threats

What Was the Free Church?

This study began with a specific question: Was the Free Church view a marginal note, a correction, or perhaps a substantive contribution in Christian history? That which is easily assumed by persons secure in the American pattern of separation of church and state is not at all self-evident within the total framework of the world Church. A major part of Christendom is still territorially defined, culturally conditioned, and to a greater or lesser degree politically controlled. Having found to his own satisfaction an answer to this question, and established some of the political and social implications of the finding, the writer was led to ask: Are the American "Free Churches" really free in the classical sense? For classical Free Churchmanship involved religious liberty in a secondary sense, whereas the primary emphasis was upon a new concept of a community of discipleship.

The rediscovery of the genius of Free Churchmanship, so useful both for Christian reform and democratic renewal, requires some review of its classical — i.e., Anabaptist/Mennonite — period. In this review we are helped considerably by the fact that Mennonite communities are still in our midst, embodying a living tradition. Although culturally conditioned and marred at points by accommodations, they can be useful in highlighting the frontiers of a renewal of the faith. The writer is grateful to report that, belonging to one of the larger and more comfortably established denominations, he has nevertheless received marked assistance from the Mennonites in defining the problem and discovering the motor of possible reform.

It has for at least a generation been clear to the fair-minded that the Anabaptists proper, the "evangelical *Taeufer*," were neither revolutionaries nor enthusiasts, prophets nor what Preserved Smith called "Bolsheviki of the sixteenth century." From the materials now at hand it further is clear that their teaching and testimony were not of marginal import but of substantive significance. Alongside the parochial pattern of medieval Catholicism, and the territorial pattern of the churches of the Reformers, must be studied the witness of those to whom the True Church was a voluntary association of convinced believers. The early Free Churchmen abhorred "culture religion," a Christendom in name only which was more accurately to be described as "baptized heathenism" (*getauftes Heidentum*). The radical Reformation, the "root-and-branch" Reformation, was in fact intended to be a *restitution* rather than a reformation. The primitive form and style of the Early Church were to be restored. With its ethical concern, its emphasis upon the normative significance of primitive Christian patterns of community life, the Restitution was as distinct from the plans of the Reformers as it was from that section of Christendom which remained obedient to the Bishop of Rome.

The Relevance of the Inquiry

There are several objective factors which contribute to the growing interest in the constitutive elements in this tradition, and in the nature of Free Church life in general. The first of these is the awareness among leaders of the old territorial churches that the Christian world-view — even in its cultural adaptations — is no longer dominant in their own areas, but has been subverted by modern secularism and openly challenged by pseudo-religions, of which Nazism and Communism have been the most demonic recent types. It is no accident that the chief spokesman for the Confessing Church should have been reported after his release from eight years of imprisonment as sceptical of the pretensions of "Christendom":

> [Martin Niemoeller] . . . said recently that he "was raised a Lutheran and did not realize that the traditional Lutheran theology regarding the State was wrong."

> He now believes that the church must exercise stronger influence on political life, as in England and the United States, where the church "acts as the conscience of the state."[2]

Recent surveys of religious loyalty in Sweden, France, Italy, and Great Britain are uniform in their findings that the collapse of the authority of old religious establishments has created (quoting John Baillie):

> . . . a situation new in the history of mankind, there being now millions of men and women in all our communities who profess no religious faith, take part in no religious observance, and have connexion with no religious institution.[3]

This "baptized heathenism" is not as new as Professor Baillie would have us believe, for it was precisely the source of much of the protest of sixteenth-century radicals (from the spiritualizer Sebastian Franck to the Anabaptist Menno Simons) against the whole idea of mass establishments. But it is new, at least, that there exist militant ideological alternatives to the faith, securely lodged in the centers of western civilization.

Significantly, Professor Baillie feels compelled to abandon the earlier coercive philosophy, which played a leading role in centuries of evangelization among the peoples of Europe.

> Such a recovered Christian civilization would clearly be of the open type which alone I am prepared to defend, and in it the older conscriptive idea of the Church's authority would have completely given place to the idea of religious freedom.[4]

That one may have a People's Church (*Volkskirche*) and at the same time an effective pattern of religious liberty is precisely the genius of the Church of Scotland.[5] But the general rule surely has been otherwise, and the degree to which plain historical trends can be reversed by rational statement of the problem is at best doubtful. In its essence, the pattern of establishment

> . . . comprehended the entire population of a parish or of a territory, implied infant baptism and coordination with the state system, and tended either toward a rigid absolutism of doctrine and authority . . . or toward a latitudinarian dilution.[6]

Neither an arid scholasticism nor a policy of promiscuous membership is adequate to missionize new territory, or even hold the line against a political pseudo-religion. It seems probable that the necessities of the case will lead more and more members of former territorial churches to a stronger view of the missionary task of the Church. In a recent ecumenical conference (Boldern, 1953), a young Swiss pastor said that he had accepted his office only with the clear understanding that the role and mission of the Church in Switzerland was precisely the same as in pre-totalitarian China. This formulation is one which the Free Church fathers would have understood and approved. The "apostasy of Christendom" is not a uniquely twentieth-century phenomenon, although it has recently assumed more violent forms.

A second factor of importance in directing attention to the principle of voluntary religious association and its expressions has been the evidence from the mission fields. When the International Missionary Council released its *Interpretative Statistical Survey of the World Mission of the Christian Church*[7] almost thirty years ago, it was already clear that the growing edge of the faith was staffed and supported primarily from the Free Churches. The premise which the Evangelical Church in Germany recently announced, that the Christian mission is the responsibility of every church member, has been an axiom of the Free Churches since the time of Anabaptists Georg Blaurock (1525) and Paul Glock (1550), and in organized form since William Carey (1792) in London and Samuel F. Mills (1810) in Boston. The future effect of this accent has been summarized by the leading contemporary historian of the expansion of Christianity:

> From the radical wing come a majority of the missionaries who are propagating Protestant Christianity in other lands. This means that the world-wide Protestantism

> of the decades ahead is probably to depart further from the Christianity of pre-Reformation days than has that of Western Europe and the British Isles. Presumably, the trend will be augmented as the "younger churches" in non-Occidental countries mount in strength.[8]

The necessary consequences of the struggle with totalitarianism in Europe, the logic of the missionary drive of the Free Churches, the growing importance of the younger churches of Asia and Africa, all serve to underline the reasons why further study of the nature of Free Church life is relevant and indeed essential.

Thirdly, the emergence of the ecumenical movement, with the accompanying discussions between representatives of the most various traditions of church order, has served to bring to light the teachings and testimonies of the Free Churches which had long been ignored or misinterpreted in older centers of western Christianity. The coming to the fore in international affairs of America, a country where the Free Church way has long been accepted, has not been without affect in the religious sphere. This has been notable in postwar Germany[9] and Japan, and in the programs of the various departments of the World Council of Churches itself. (Even the Roman Catholic Church — consider the recent fiery exchange between Cardinal Segura of Spain and the American Jesuit scholars — has not remained uninfluenced by the obvious example of a New World in which religious confession and civic rights are two distinct spheres.)

The ecumenical movement, with its emphasis upon encounter and discussion aimed toward consensus, is peculiarly open to the Free Church way of doing things. Co-operation, re-union can come about only through the guidance of the Holy Spirit working in the midst. Emphasis upon some particular tradition of churchly rite (such as the objective validity of Sacramental forms, central to Catholicism), or upon some unique dogmatic formulation (as in the Concordiae Reformatorum, central to territorial Protestantism), can only divide. Here is a very direct reason why those in the Anabaptist/Mennonite tradition should not hesitate to join in fair and frank encounters with all who are willing to let their thoughts and actions be influenced by brotherly admonition, exhortation, common prayer, joint study.

What Is the Church?

The key query, which alone justifies comparative study and discussion, and on which the Free Church way ultimately must stand or fall, is this: "What is the Church?" This is a query which cannot be answered by history or sociology, although both disciplines can illuminate the debate; we are led back to basic Biblical and theological premises which are central to the faith. From past experience Free Church bodies are inclined to believe that their chief struggle must still be directed against establishments, and sometimes this may still be true — as in Italy or Spain under the Concordats. But within the area of influence of the ecumenical movement this is no longer true. A revealing little incident is connected with the history of the Bad Boll annual conferences sponsored by the Stuttgart Ecumenical Committee for the last several years in southern Germany (annually since 1951). The first year the conference was announced as one between *"The Church* and the *Free-churches";* since then the title has been, "The *Land-church* and the *Free Church."* In such subtle ways may a revolution in thought be announced.

The basic threats to the integrity of the Church today are two: from the various expressions of totalitarianism, and from the spiritualizers who claim some general relationship to the Christian movement but reject the yoke of the Lord.[10] These challenges are both more serious by far for the future of our Free Church way than is the older form of establishment. Religious toleration is not, to be sure, religious liberty; but the friendly benevolence of a Bishop Dibelius toward the Free Churches contrasts markedly with the malevolence of a Pieck or Grotewohl (in the Communist part of the same city, Berlin) towards all forms of the Christian mission.

A territorial church, particularly of the type governed by an ecclesiastical monarch, may reach very satisfactory arrangements with a totalitarian form of government. The 1929 Lateran agreement between Mussolini and the Vatican, and the 1933 Concordat between Hitler and the Vatican — both of which are still in effect — illustrate the point.[11] A Free Church, however, with its necessary refusal to acknowledge the right of the state either to persecute or to sponsor, with its independent centers of ethical opinion, with its missionary drive, can only resist totalitarianism or betray its calling. When Bishop Otto Melle of the German Methodist Episcopal Church achieved peace with the Nazis by reducing the congregations for which he was responsible to pietist conventicles, he betrayed the Church. Today, in Communist controlled areas, the Christian churches confront a similar choice between *Gleichschaltung* and persecution for the faith's sake.

The oblique challenge of the spiritualizers is generally more serious in those areas where toleration or religious liberty has spared the Church from persecution. The totalitarians have, however, made skillful use of such disintegrative factors in their warfare on the Christian Church. From Pilgram Marpeck (1495?-1556) to John Wesley (1703-1791), the great figures of Free Church history have had little use for the "I" = centeredness of mysticism, for the prideful individualism which slights the means of grace; they have certainly had no patience with cultists with special revelations to peddle. It is revealing that a recent review of the Quaker situation should conclude:

> Encouraged by the educational and political doctrines of the times many Friends have come to look to the individual as the center of the universe. . . . Conscience has replaced the old concept of the Inner Christ and each man decides for himself.[12]

The mature prayer is *common* prayer: "Give *us* . . . Forgive *us* . . . Lead *us* not . . . Deliver *us*. . . ."

> For what we preach is not ourselves, but Jesus Christ as Lord, with ourselves as your servants for Jesus' sake.
>
> For it is the God who said, "Let Light shine out of

darkness," who has shone in our hearts to give the light of the knowledge of the glory of God in the face of Christ (II Cor. 4:5-6).

To the average American, in his matter-of-fact way and ready association in co-operative efforts along many lines, the sticky experimentalism of individualistic inspiration is less appealing, however, than an uncertain appeal to collective wisdom. He is more vulnerable to contemporary gnosticism than to individual mysticism. Thus Gerald Heard, who has enjoyed a certain popularity among some intellectuals, proclaims that the chief need of today is

> . . . to restate religion in modern language . . . to make it an instrument whereby the sundered self-conscious individual re-binds himself to the common Eternal Life flowing in his fellows, in all creatures and in all creation.[13]

Such a statement is expansively vague enough to sound appealing; besides, it appears to have intellectual sophistication!

Without going into further detail on a matter which must be treated later under its proper heading, as a manifestation of culture religion (the "American religion"), it is important to note here that the chief challenges to the integrity of the Church today are precisely those in encountering which the Anabaptist testimony took its classical form: in surviving persecution, and in eliminating spiritualizing tendencies.[14]

A student of the early generations of the faith has portrayed the Church in competition with the alternatives:

> The Christian *Ecclesia* is best appreciated when observed at work in an intensely religious world in competition with the Synagogues of the Dispersion, the Guilds of the Mystery-Religions, and the Schools of Greek Philosophy.[15]

The credal pronouncements, the decision on church order, can best be understood in terms of the Church's struggle with her enemies, both without and within. This was true of the Early Church, true of the Free Church fathers of the sixteenth century, and will be true today in so far as she is true to her Lord. No Caesar-cult ever exacted a more definite response than that whose chief shrine is the mausoleum of Lenin and Stalin in Moscow.[16] No mystery religion, or system of private inspiration of ancient times, threw a longer shadow across the Church than certain types of twentieth-century gnosticism.[17]

The Church in the Biblical World-View

The re-establishment of our continuity as Christians within the frame of reference reported and anticipated in the Old and New Testaments is a peculiarly difficult exercise for the modern mind.

> Men have always lived in "modern" times but they have not always been as much impressed with the fact. Our own time, conventionally considered as beginning about 1500 A.D., is the first to coin so neat a term and apply it so consistently. . . . The awareness of a shared newness, of a way of life different from that of one's forebears — and by 1700 awareness of a way of life felt by many to be much *better* than that of their forebears — this is in itself one of the clearest marks of our modern culture.[18]

Quite evidently that millennialist style of politics which abandons *anno Domini,* in favor of the Year 1 of the Fascist or Nazi or Communist Revolution, has deeper roots in our common intellectual and emotional heritage than most of us care to admit.

Protestants have brought upon themselves the lack of a sense of tradition, in part, by neglecting those periods which lay between the Reformation and the Early Church. The scurrilous pamphlet circulated by Roman Catholic tractarians in the United States Armed Forces, dating the Catholic Church from Jesus Christ and the Protestants from Martin Luther (1517), did not jar our subconscious as much as it should have. Yet we are, in the meaning of the Christian canon, children of the Covenant: heirs with Abraham of the promises recorded in the seventeenth chapter of Genesis, heirs with the first Christians of the fulfillment in the Living Word "written not with ink but with the Spirit of the Living God, not on tablets of stone but on tablets of the human heart" (II Cor. 3:3). The writer of Hebrews believed that the promise found in Jeremiah 31:31-34 was fulfilled in the new community of believers. "They shall be to me a people" (Hebr. 8:10; Jer. 31:33).

In the diaspora congregations, where Christian life made the first break from Jewish sectarianism toward universalism, the Christians were God's flock, a household, God's own people, a spiritual house (I Pet., *passim*).[19] This social relationship in the Old Testament between members of the congregation was in no sense based upon the natural emergence of a tribal order: the covenant and the law were founded in a Divine act of grace, in a special revelation of God.[20]

The social relationship in the New Testament is centered likewise in a Covenant, founded in the mission of the Messiah who is the crucified and risen Lord.

> . . . God is Father and King of his people, not of isolated individuals.
>
> In the same way, the risen Lord is Lord of his people, and the thought that faith in Christ leaves fellowship in the Church optional would have been rejected by the New Testament Christians as a startling mistake. We have often taken the Pauline phrase "in Christ" to be nothing more than the expression of individualistic mysticism. This is radically wrong; it is a view which springs from modern individualism and Greek attitudes rather than from a true understanding of the Apostle. He is clear that to be "in Christ," while it is a great personal experience and privilege, is a privilege which inevitably puts a man into the Church and binds him to his fellow-believers in the one "body of Christ" (I Cor. 12:27), of which the risen Christ is the living Head (Col. 1:18; Eph. 1:22f).
>
> Similarly the Holy Spirit is a Church-building, fellowship-building power. In Acts the Spirit comes to groups of believers, not to self-sufficient individuals.[21]

"Togetherness" is a constant refrain (Phil. 2:1; II Cor. 13:13). In the Bible history is real; it has a beginning, a meaning and direction, and an end. And this is a more radical break from non-Christian philosophies and religions (though not from Judaism) than we are likely to remember at first, particularly in a time of domineering secular eschatologies.

In the Church which followed on Christ's resurrection the Holy Spirit resides and rules as counselor and witness to the Truth (John 16:5-15). Here is no prophetism or individual inspiration, no bag of individual grains of sand, but a corporate entity of such intensely binding quality that the metaphor of a living body springs repeatedly to the lips. In the Anabaptist sense of joint responsibility (and not in the modern sense of individual rights and prerogatives, adapted from the sphere of political rights), discipleship was marked by the Covenant of a good conscience with God (I Pet. 3:21). With the launching of the historic mission of the Christian Church after Pentecost, salvation is inextricably bound up with obedience to the guidance of the Holy Spirit in a realm of which Christ is the Lord.

> First: the Holy Spirit is henceforth a corporate, not an individual possession. Church and Holy Spirit are from this point on inseparable. . . . Apart from this corporate community, there is no gift of the Holy Spirit.[22]

One can hardly conceive of a more radical antithesis to early or late gnosticism, with its emphasis upon a secret knowledge which supersedes the Christian revelation; or a more radical antithesis to early or late spiritualizing, which substitutes a direct illumination of the individual conscience for the disciplines of the community of the faithful. If the Reformers enthroned the principle of the individual conscience, which is doubtful, the Anabaptists did not; and in this they were true to the work of the Christ and the historical function of the Christian Church. With them the individual person shared in the priesthood, and brought his word and conscience to the common table; but he did not exist as an isolate.

The nature of the Covenant, in its several forms, and of the mission of the Church for the world, was rooted and grounded in a teaching which is almost as offensive to the modern individualist as the above doctrine of the Church: namely, the doctrine of the election of a Messiah-people who carry history. Both Israel and "the new Israel" were, in their time, a "chosen" people. The doctrine of election and the universal perspectives of the faith were not at odds, but rather dialectically related, complementary to each other. Israel was chosen not by merit and not in favoritism, but in terms of the Divine purpose for the world. In concluding a great study of this relationship, Professor H. H. Rowley summarizes:

> This Biblical doctrine of election may be proclaimed without apology and its proclamation is greatly to be desired to yield the foundation of a revived doctrine of the Church.[23]

Here again we are brought to the centrality of the doctrine of the Church, the role of the community of disciples that knows a Truth which the world repudiates and worships a Savior whom the world crucified. This is a "high" doctrine of the Church; it was, moreover, also confessed by the Anabaptists.

The tension between "the Church" and "the world" is of the nature of Christian history. In the Roman Empire, Christ could have shared the pantheon with other gods, had he been "tolerant" and not "jealous."[24] The Free Church fathers might have been accepted had they not made such unreasonable demands for the community of discipleship that Christendom could not contain them. The Church today finds ready acceptance by totalitarians and spiritualizers alike when it accommodates itself to the norms set from outside; i.e., when it ceases to be the Church. But the refusal to accommodate, to forswear its divine mission and historic claim, is precisely the root of the offense.

The implementation of the mission of the Church requires in each period of history a certain discipline, intellectual and ethical. Above all, the life of the Church in warfare with competing creeds and patterns of life is characterized by a certain "style" of operation. There was a wide variety of church order in the early years, and considerable leeway was given to fresh insights within the life of the fellowship.

> This is of course clearest in St. Paul, who thought of church government as a rather inferior office, and who ranked the gifts of healing, teaching, and even perhaps speaking with tongues and interpreting them, as superior to it (I Cor. 12:8-10, and 28). We have a natural abhorrence of prophets, and hardly think of them as men particularly fitted to rule our great denominations; but in the early church they were venerated next to apostles themselves.
>
> Orders do not validate the Church, the Church validates them.[25]

The essential matter for the Church is neither a particular type of order nor a unique formulation of doctrine. It is rather the cultivation of that frame of mind and readiness of action which makes for a quickened response to the will and guidance of her Lord. This will is made known to the community through common prayer, discussion, study, joint action. It is rooted in the Bible record of God's work among men; it is nourished by the means of grace; it is pruned by preaching and teaching. But its unique "style," from the Free Church point of view, is in the cultivation of those interpersonal relationships which produce a consensus. Of decision in the Church it is reported, not that a majority ruled, but that "... it seemed good to the Holy Spirit and to us." (Acts 15:28.)

The actual attaining of a consensus may, of course, be difficult in the immediate. Some months ago a church history appointment was to be made in a European theological school. The appointment belongs to the church, and is voted in assembly. On the first vote the two leading candidates paired at 375 to 375. Six month later, when the matter had been subject to further prayer and discussion, the vote was

362 to 362. One is reminded of the quip of the Commonwealth Period that the Holy Spirit is "the odd man." Generally, however, the Holy Spirit lets His will be more clearly discerned. In any case the holding of votes is a mere tactic of approximation: the "talking up" which precedes a decision, whether a vote is taken in parliamentary form or not, is the essence of the matter.

In this also the Anabaptists brought a restitution of apostolic Christian life. The laity came into its own again, in a community of priesthood. In thus cutting through to the heart of the matter, in restoring to supremacy the first of all Christian disciplines — the practice of brotherhood — the Free Churches may today not only recover an essential part of their own heritage but carry a much needed testimony to brethren in other folds and to a world sick with division and strife.

II. How the Free Church Emerged

The Christendom of Rome and the Reformers

The particular relationship of church and state in the Middle Ages, and the role of the Christian communities in pre-Reformation society, lie outside the scope of this study. We are directed to an interpretation of the Free Church history and testimony. A year after the discovery of America it was still possible for the Papacy to claim the right to divide the New World between two colonial powers (1493). Within the next half century, however, those who called — for various reasons — for a reformation of the power structure within Christendom, had generally abandoned hope of establishing a representative system (by use of Councils of the Church) and many were in open revolt against overcentralization of power in the Church. In most of northern Europe the right of Christian laymen, at least those in positions of political authority, to carry through measures aimed at spiritual improvement of the Church was openly asserted. Dissatisfaction with a power concentration in the Papacy had spread also to dissatisfaction with a class monopoly of the "Roman Doctors" (lawyers and theologians). In the process of developing the protest, not only the temporal but also the spiritual claims of the Bishop of Rome were voided in large areas.

The encyclical *Unam Sanctam* of Boniface VIII (1302) had asserted the Roman claim:

> We declare, affirm, define and pronounce that it is altogether necessary to salvation for every human creature to be subject to the Roman pontiff.[1]

The sixteenth-century protest was not the first objection to the political and spiritual implications of the Bishop's demand for submission. This claim, with its political implementation, had met recurring opposition from linguistic, cultural, pre-national elements within the Holy Roman Empire which were not willing to yield to centralization. One of the most striking early protests was that of the Donatists in the time of Augustine. (The Anabaptists were later to be compared with the Donatists, chiefly by their enemies.) The extent to which the religious issue was compromised by nontheological factors has led one student to put the problem as a question:

> How far was the struggle between Orthodoxy and Heresy, in the later Roman Empire, really a political struggle between the central authorities of the Empire and the different nations of which the Empire was composed?[2]

The triumph of Latin over the vernacular (Punic or German, as the case may be) may have been important to Rome, but it was hard for a non-Roman to perceive its justification in Scripture. When Luther asserted the independence of his "good Germans" from transalpine authority he was carrying on an old tradition. There are some who for romantic or apologetic reasons glorify the Middle Ages and what they term "the break-up of Christendom." Historically minded persons should not forget that the peculiar mixture of national and religious interest which strengthened the hands of the Reformers was opposed to another, centralized, mixture of religious and political interests which was dominated by Rome.

The argument entered by Stephen Gardiner, Bishop of Winchester, in his *De vera obedientia* (c. 1534), was congenial to Reformers on the Continent as well as in England:

> The Church is . . . an amalgam of functions analogous to those proper to the practice of medicine or to a university; this being so, she must be entirely subject to the King's will.[3]

Gardiner's description of the Church was a true one for pre-

Reformation Christendom as well; only the element of royal authority was added. The principle *quod principi placuit, legis habet vigorem* ("what pleased the prince has the force of law") resulted in the religio-sociological sphere in *cuius regio, eius religio* ("whoever rules determines the religion of his subjects," in free translation). The Augsburg Religious Peace (1555) recognized, in fact, a principle of government which was as acceptable to the Roman Catholic authorities as to the new Protestants. "Caesero-Papism" was in practice, if not asserted as boldly in theory, in areas loyal to the Papacy as well as in areas dominated by the Reformers.

The protest of the radical Reformers (the Anabaptists, the party of the Restitution), on the other hand, was directed against all articulation of the territorial principle in the domain of the Church and Her Lord. The sixteenth century saw an expansion of Roman law rather than a decline, and also of the juristic bureaucracy which implemented it, into Protestant areas. Both civil and church processes were affected. The peasants, in their revolt (1525-26), demanded the elimination of the influence of the "Roman Doctors" and a return to the old ways of Germanic tribal virtue.

The religious radicals were likewise a popular movement, opposed to carefully codified systems of religious law and thought — whether such codes were used to assert the authority of the Roman pontiff or the divine right of kings. In the Holy Homan Empire of the whole people the Church had come to be, for all practical purposes, the clergy.[4] In spite of Luther's teaching about "the priesthood of all believers," the state church Reformers did not, according to the Anabaptists, basically alter the pattern. What still remained unperformed by the "halfway men" (as the Free Church fathers called the Reformers) was a thoroughgoing restitution of the life and spirit of the New Testament Church. The claims of the Protestant princes, with their territorial churches, were not markedly better than the political claims of the Bishop of Rome — in so far as the nature of the Church was concerned.

The coming of the Reformation did not bring, in short,

any immediate decline of the concept of *Corpus Christianum,* although it introduced more open divisions into it. Luther and Calvin both thought in terms of complementary territorial and religious institutions, and both were bitterly opposed to any pluralism of religious communities within a given territory. The problems of securing the liberty of preaching, of maintaining a church order, of providing a system of inspection, were variously answered by the Reformers. But they one and all finally came to the conclusion that such discipline as had to be exercised should be in the old medieval way through the magistrates, and not in any "new" fashion borrowed from the primitive Church.

The Reformers were not untroubled by the vision of the Church at Jerusalem, to be sure. Zwingli and Calvin both were inspired by the vision of the Early Church, but shied away from steps toward a radical Restitution. Oecolampadius once attempted to restore the ban as a practice of primitive church government, but abandoned it. Martin Butzer's indirect influence on the Genevan order involved the rediscovery of the ban, and reflected the order which Jakob Sturm had introduced in the Strassburg churches to meet the Anabaptist challenge.[5] But the ultimate disciplinary authority in Geneva continued to rest with the Town Council, which on at least one occasion even assumed authority to grant absolution to a district which had been placed under Roman Catholic excommunication.[6] Leo Jud, Zwingli's collaborator and successor, was much concerned for the freedom of preaching, and eventually drifted away from the cantonal standing order. Splitting later with Heinrich Bullinger, he came under Schwenckfeld's influence and lived to die in exile in south Germany.[7] Johannes Brenz was opposed to persecution for inner faith, but said that if the dissidents erected a public order they should either be required to produce miracles like the apostles or be put down by the authorities.[8] Thus one Reformer after another, however tempted, drew back before the logic of a radical New Testament order. It is surely wrong to attribute to any one of them an attitude of religious voluntaryism which modern countries largely take for granted as a right. The Reformers can hardly be cited to support religious liberty, and were horrified by the implications of the Free Church position.

It has been argued by a Catholic liberal that Protestantism was especially prone to persecution, since it allowed the state to enter into matters of faith.[9] So much for theory. In practice both Roman Catholicism and state church Protestantism deferred to political authorities in the various lands. Only in England and America did the pattern of religious freedom develop out of the Free Church principles. When it came back to the Continent, where the sixteenth-century pioneers left no continuing congregations, it came largely as a consequence of the Enlightenment — by reason of the disintegration of Christendom rather than through its radical transformation. It is interesting to speculate what the history of western Europe might have been had a thoroughgoing reformation taken place. The various Reformers, in their time, not without some inward struggle, were unable to conceive of a church order which would establish the break from Rome and not come to terms with the political authorities which had made such a break possible. "Where God sets a Church the devil builds a chapel" — this was their view of the radical Restitution.

It remained for a later period of territorial Protestantism, softened by the Enlightenment and attacked by secular enemies, to begin to perceive that there was substantive merit in the Free Church position. The Anabaptist testimony was, moreover, in its own time blackened by a supposed connection with the bloody revolution of the peasants and the craftsmen (Thomas Müntzer), and with the inspired social and religious prophets (Melchior Hofmann, Hans Hut, Augustin Bader, David Joris). The Belgic Confession of the Reformed tradition doubtless sums up the conclusions of the Reformers generally concerning the radical stand:

> We detest the Anabaptists and other seditious people, and in general all those who reject the higher powers and magistrates and would subvert justice, introduce community of goods, and confound that decency and good order which God has established among men.

Only recently could a scholar in that tradition — and not without protest from some of his fellow churchmen — distinguish between detesting "Anabaptists" and detesting "Anabaptism," the latter also doubtful.[10]

The documents clearly show, however, that the state church investigators were capable of distinguishing in court between those who adhered to revolutionary Münster, those who belonged to the voluntary communist communities in Moravia, and those who were simple Bible-believing folk. But both revolutionaries and Moravian Hutterites appeared to be communists, or sympathetic to them (an opinion as disreputable in the sixteenth century as in the twentieth), and in any case subversive of good order in society and in Christendom. The Edict of January 4, 1528, and the Imperial Mandate of April 23, 1529, which Charles V issued for suppression of the Anabaptists,[11] the general decision to make the old law of Justinian against the rebaptizers applicable to the radicals, were — as it finally worked out — as representative of established Protestant judgment as of Roman Catholic.

As late as 1855 (Eisenach), in fact, the Evangelical Church in Germany felt free to define "the Church" as a religious body possessing political privileges, a bland assumption lying just beneath the surface in Ernst Troeltsch and Karl Holl and still encountered in more backward Continental church circles.

Modifications in the British Pattern

The closest approach in Reformation time to complete religious liberty, in which the various parties were to agree to differ in religious matters and combine in civic concerns, occurred under the Protectorate (1653-60) in England. The earliest example of the *pax dissidentium* had been in Poland, in 1573, when Protestant groups who frankly differed in confession and church order covenanted together to keep the peace — shedding no blood, imposing no penalties, confiscating no goods for diversity in faith and practice. But the Jesuit Counter-Reformation destroyed this plan, and the disappearance of the Polish Minor Church put an end to one of the most romantic and little-known chapters of Free Church history. Oliver Cromwell, who desired even the weakest and meanest to know him only as "Lord Protector," abandoned the concept of a Christian Commonwealth with religion established by the state for that of a limited state exercising a benevolent patronage to several churches on equal footing. The sects destroyed his plan, and English policy has continued to this day as *toleration* under an Establishment, rather than *liberty*.

The Reformation in England was not initially a popular movement, but through the experiences of the Commonwealth and the Evangelical Awakening eventually penetrated much more deeply than it has in several of the Continental lands to the present day. As in the Lutheran and Calvinist reformations, separation of the Church from the state was in no sense intended by the Anglican or Presbyterian reformers. The Church of England, of whom the sovereign has been *summus episcopos* from the father of Elizabeth I to Elizabeth II, enjoyed a reformation which penetrated the homes of individual members only with the generation of John Wesley. The Presbyterian party from the beginning equally discountenanced disestablishment. The initial break from Rome, stamped by the politics of the king, was to be carried through by a frank use of patronage under the guidance of members of the clergy.

> The Archbishop and Bishops, Archdeacons and ministers were to be each assisted in Church government by eight or twelve persons (pastors, deacons, "grave and godly men of worship," i.e. laymen, and perhaps justices of the peace). These were to be appointed by the assemblies of the Church, which could be developed with little trouble from the gatherings of the clergy usual at the various visitations.[12]

Unlike the Separatists, whose first little congregations accepted exile in Holland and sometimes in America rather than concourse with an established church, the Presbyterians fought for a church order which could join hands with the Scots in delivering Britain to the Reformed order.

> Either must we have a right ministerie of God, & a right government of his church, according to the Scriptures set up (bothe whiche we lacke) or else there can be no right religion, nor yet for contempt therof can Gods plagues be from us any while deferred.[13]

When Puritan congregations went to New England, whose early church order was more Genevan than in most Reformed lands, they did not look back upon England's standing order as a swamp of iniquities but with eyes of affectionate regret. One of their early martyrs, punished with amputation of the right hand, raised the bloody stump and cried out: "God save the Queen!" But the spokesman of the Anglican party, Bishop Matthew Parker, the party which in fact enjoyed the favor of the Queen, could only exclaim: God keep us from such things as Knocks have attempted in Scotland: the people are orderers of all things. The popular party of a later date, to whom "new presbyter" was but "old Priest writ large," succeeded only temporarily in gaining power; complete toleration of Free Churches came fairly late to Great Britain. We are today apt to forget, with Britain's liberal scheme of toleration before us, that as late as 1880, persons not members of the Church of England could take no degrees at Cambridge or Oxford.

Nevertheless, there were from an early date meliorative factors at work in the English scene. Where the Scots had the convenient myth that Robert the Bruce (1274-1329) fought and established a limited, contractural community, a myth which neatly fitted the Calvinist doctrine of the role of the magistrates, Englishmen had their rights at common law. Whereas on the Continent the influence of politics on religion worked to strengthen the structure of authority within the churches, in England the struggle for political liberties complemented the fight for religious freedom. The day came on the Continent when in reaction to established powers the militant social and political forces were almost by definition anti-clerical and frequently anti-Christian. In

England the most progressive social forces and parties have grown out of the churches, out of nonconformity and an Anglican order purified by competition with it.

In the year 1616 occurred an incident symbolic of the different Continental and English developments. A case was brought before the high court which involved the king's prerogative, and James I forbade that the matter be judged. Relying upon the Roman legal concept of the king as the source of law, he considered the judges to be "lions under the throne." All submitted, except the Lord Chief Justice, Sir Edward Coke. Coke stated boldly that he would resign rather than let that doctrine stand: the king was subject to the Constitution of the land the same as any other man. The death of Charles I thirty-three years later is witness to the fact that the Stuarts learned the lesson with difficulty. But from Coke's stand to equal justice under the law is but a step, and from equal justice to the Levellers' plea that "the poorest he that is in England hath a life to live as the richest he." In contrast with those lands where the triumph of Roman law places the subjects, even today, in a position of response to sovereign action transmitted by bureaucracies which once represented the will of princes, the articulation of the general will has become in England the culmination of free and informed discussions pointing toward a consensus. It has been the English experience that the open forum ill accords with the system of coercion of conscience which is a thoroughgoing religious establishment.

Christendom Today

In England the established church gradually lost her political power before the logic of common law development. On the Continent, it took the erosion of revolutionary secularism to accomplish the same result. Today, when one surveys the map of religious liberty, and thereby the status of the Church or churches, it is plain that there are two chief sources of coercion remaining: totalitarian Communism, and governments in those Roman Catholic countries which still retain the doctrine and practice of the old view of Christendom. Delaying our discussion of political oppression for a later chapter, we may note that there are three chief locations of religious persecution of the type which marred the state church, both Protestant and Roman Catholic, in the sixteenth century: Colombia (Free Churches, .25%), Italy (.35%), and Spain (.10%). According to agreement between Franco and the Vatican, Protestants in Spain presently suffer under the following disabilities:

> 1. Our children are obliged to receive Roman Catholic religious instruction, and also to be present at Mass. No Protestant schools are allowed.
> 2. We have no right to publish our own papers, or our own works of theology, or even our own hymn books.
> 3. Our own members are not allowed to contract a civil marriage although they have been baptised into the Roman Church.
> 4. Spanish Protestants are not allowed access to various posts under the State on the pretext that the State is Roman Catholic. We ask that the religious beliefs of our people should be respected. . . . We ask for the right of burying our dead according to our own faith, and of celebrating a religious service at the graveside, and we want to be sure that in districts where the civil cemetery does not exist that a corner may be reserved where we may bury our dear ones in a place which is perfectly suitable.[14]

More recently, even American citizens resident in Spain have had their rights abridged with the complicity of their own government.

In Protestant areas, on the other hand, the old coercive pattern of the territorial church privilege has largely been abandoned. On January 1, 1952, a law was passed giving every Swedish citizen the right freely to exercise his religion; Free Church and Roman Catholic marriages are to be recognized.[15] In the German Republic the postwar constitution guarantees religious freedom to every citizen, although the established churches still enjoy state support for training their ministers and teachers, and the use of the government tax machinery in collecting church tithes. In the Russian Zone of Germany the churches have been partially disestablished. Every report from the Soviet Zone emphasizes that the members have shown a new and unexpected loyalty which underlines the old Anabaptist claim that separation of church and state is good for the Church. Political benefits are secondary, and may not be evident for a time.

The intervention of the King of Norway in a dispute over Hell and its properties has precipitated an acute crisis in the Church of Norway; Bishop Rangvald Indebro of Bjorgvin has predicted the end of the state church if the state does not retract from its insistence on priority in settling religious disputes.

In Great Britain, where the refusal of Parliament to amend the Book of Common Prayer excited widespread discussion in 1928, the topic of total disestablishment has been in the news frequently in recent years. In any case, opinion has shifted to a point not far from the logic of the Free Church position; a thorough study of the religious state of England a decade ago concluded, among other things:

> Up to the present, those called to the ministry of the Church have been trained with a pastoral, rather than an evangelistic office in view. The assumption that the Church is coterminous with the nation, upon which the parochial organization is based, seems to persist though it is no longer true.[16]

The members of the study group went on to suggest an approach to the task of the Church which certainly commends itself to Free Churchmen as strongly as to Anglicans.

The major Protestant establishments today are characterized, in short, by a readiness to accept change and to discuss the merits of the case for religious liberty. This fact should serve as a challenge to the Free Churches to prove their case.

The Radical Testimony

The last four centuries have seen major Christian protest of three types, all present in the sixteenth century and all known to us today. These are:

1. the revolutionary type ("Maccabean Christianity") such as that of Thomas Müntzer,
2. the spiritualizers,
3. "integral" Christianity of the classical Free Church style; the Restitution of the True Church.

"Maccabean Christianity" (The Revolutionaries)

Thomas Müntzer has been acclaimed variously by Social Democratic historians such as Belfort Bax and Karl Kautsky as a presocialist revolutionary, and by the apologists for the Third Reich as a forerunner of National Socialism. His reputation is today being reconditioned in Communist East Germany. In one thing the Nazis had the advantage, for Müntzer had a small private income and was not a member of the proletariat.[17] At first attached to the Lutheran party, he was led by his conviction of personal contact with God and temperamental impatience with the more slowly moving Reformers to take direct action against the old order. With great power to sway crowds of people (even in the revolt of the peasants his role was that of agitator rather than organizer), he proclaimed at Alstedt the founding of a communist *Bund;* a community of saints was to be gathered in these last days, and the godless Canaanites slain. He began with a theme very widespread among the radicals at the time: that the old Church had fallen through the profiteering and corruption of the priestly class.

> I have read often and much the history of the Old Fathers. I find the Church of Christ spotless and a virgin up to the death of the disciples of the Apostles.[18]

But of more fatal significance than his Christian primitivism was Müntzer's sense that the last days were at hand, with the setting aright of ancient social and economic wrongs.

> You see, our Lords and Princes are the dregs of profiteering, thievery and robbery; they take everything for their property. The fish in the water, the birds in the

> air, the crops of the land — all must be theirs. Then they let out God's Law among the poor, and say: God commanded, thou shalt not steal! But they do not consider this commandment binding on themselves.[19]

The "Fall" had not only occurred in the Church. Like Karl Marx later, and Gerard Winstanley before Marx, Müntzer declared that there had been a "Fall" in society with the introduction of the Roman law of private property. In the golden time of primitive virtue, all had been held in common; with the restoration of the true way in the final Age, old rights would be regained. His seal and banner are revealing:

> The Banner is the sign of the new Covenant, in which God, as once in the apostolic times, would again speak directly with his elect in visions and dreams; the red Cross and the white Sword on it proclaim that the Elect have the right and the duty to destroy the godless with force.[20]

He died by the sword which he had raised, at Mühlhausen, in Thuringia, in the slaughter of the peasant forces; and ever thereafter, when someone mentioned Anabaptists or intentional fellowship to Martin Luther, the great Reformer recoiled from the shadow of Thomas Müntzer — as Augustine had before him developed a doctrine of persecution out of his experience with the Donatist *Circumcelliones.*

Less than a decade later the banner of revolution was raised over the city of Münster in Westphalia (1534-35). And again a Lutheran preacher, Bernt Rothmann, was the agitator at the center of it. Much of the preaching throughout north Germany which prepared the way for the streaming of thousands toward the new Jerusalem was done by Melchior Hofmann and Melchior Rinck — both of them by tradition disciples of Thomas Müntzer, and both of them declared prophets of the last days. And both, like Müntzer and Rothmann, were originally partisans of the Lutheran cause. Rothmann, preacher in the key church of the city, had been won by the "Wassenberger preachers" to the conclusion that the godly must be gathered in community apart from the godless. The restitution of primitive virtue in an earthly city should herald the Coming Again of Christ and the general establishment of His Kingdom on Earth. And in this restitution, several virtues were acquired: among them, the right understanding of the promises in the Book, promises previously hidden to the learned; the restoration of true baptism, of belief and confession rather than the false washing of children; the restitution of the True Church, that had been "falsified and hindered by the Pope and his hangers-on through fourteen hundred years";[21] the establishment of community of goods among the living communion of saints; the institution of the right plan of holy matrimony (polygamy, as in the Old Testament). They called their king "David," and themselves a new Israel, and distributed *The Book of Wrath* (Rothmann) throughout the countryside:

> God will provide his People with iron bugles and bronze claws; for Babylon must be destroyed; yea, the oxen and cattle must be slaughtered and the birds killed, before one can come properly to the wedding. Truly God will come down from heaven but the knights of God must first let loose wrath, and put down the authority of the unrighteous. . . . The humble weapons of the Apostles must be left lying where they have fallen, and the mighty armor of David be put on.[22]

The seal of Jan of Leyden, "King David," had a globe at the center transfixed by a sword. Philip of Hesse, generally a tolerator, joined his with the forces of the Roman Catholic bishop to starve out the city. The bones of the leaders of the rebellion hung in iron cages on the tower of St. Lambert's Church into the nineteenth century.

In the Commonwealth period in England, the radical groups again show the curious parallelism in thinking between the restitution of a Fallen Church and a Fallen Society. As the original model of the Church was the first age of Christianity, so the English nation had its model. The myth of the "noble Saxon," combined with a hatred of all "Norman" influence, was used as a whip against degeneracy in the prelacy and in the nation. With the breaking forth of the Reformation there was the greatest opportunity in six hundred years to make England a free and happy nation.[23] For the Fifth Monarchy Men, it was the time of the final restoration of all things:

> Obj: But Christ saith, *My Kingdom is not of this world.* How then can it now be expected?
>
> R: But he doth not say, It shall not be upon the earth, nor while the earth remains (see the contrary, Rev. 5.10). But *world* is taken for the time of continuance of that worldly government. The world is put for the Roman monarchy (Luke 2.1): When the fifth monarchy begins, shall be those new heavens and new earth spoken of (Heb. 2.5.).[24]

This is the authentic revolutionary note, based not upon a moderate or radical reform within history but upon the Joachimite expectancy of the end of history. The Independents and Baptists and Quakers, as continuing communities of faith, had to work out their teaching and discipline in part on the borderline against this type of chiliasm.

In our own time, revolutionary ideology has become largely separated from the religious frame of reference. Both Nazism and Communism have their own schemes of redemption and salvation, and qualify as "religions" in their own right. It is worth noting, however, that in the Jehovah's Witnesses we have a dispensation in the true "Maccabean" line. And although recent conventions in the United States have given some signs that the movement is settling into the lines of a fairly stable cult, the rapid growth during the first postwar years in middle Europe indicated the peculiar suitability of its appeal to situations of strain and stress.

Here again the primitivist motif was evident. The occupants of Bethel House, the communal headquarters in Brooklyn, can refer to their communism of consumption as that of a "primitive Christian community."

Rutherford himself asserted that his movement had

recovered "the original Christian basis" of religion. Exemplifying this return to "original Christianity," the literature has consistently appealed to ancient manuscripts of the Bible rather than to the "inferior" common versions. This appeal attracts many who yearn for a return to the true religion of Jesus. As one Witness said after her first visit to a Company meeting: "This meeting was the nearest approach in its character to the New Testament idea of the assembling of the saints that I have ever seen or heard."

> This stress on primitivism is also found in Mr. Rutherford's claim that the way of life pictured in the Old Testament indicates the will of Jehovah for the perfect society of the future. Rutherford described the future state as the time when every man would "sit under his own tree" and enjoy the fruits of his labor. The same nostalgia for the ancient past moves those with whom present-day society has dealt harshly.[25]

The use of the Old Testament in such context is itself revealing. The Witnesses, like their spiritual forebears in Münster, have never been New Testament nonresisters; they plead their case against bearing arms for worldly governments on the ground that they can only fight in the coming Kingdom. And like those who sallied forth to die before the beleaguered city walls of Münster, they sing hymns in the face of persecution:

> The Witnesses have always felt that a positive sign of the coming end of the age was the banning of their movement by all nations. The crushing of the Jehovah's Witnesses in Germany with the rise to power of Adolf Hitler had an electrifying effect upon the morale of the Witnesses in this country. Instead of feeling discouraged they rejoiced and looked forward with eager anticipation to similar actions in other countries. When Australia and Canada barred the organization, the Witnesses in this country took further hope that the age was fast closing. Now they are almost jubilantly anticipating the closing of the movement by the government of the United States. In such an eventuality the Wit-

nesses feel that the Kingdom would be very close at hand.[26]

Although the churches find little occasion to take the Witnesses as a serious theological or organizational threat, a second look at the unchurched of our American cities and countryside would reveal that the Witnesses' energy and willingness to sacrifice is steadily gaining converts. Any national disaster, which would heighten the appeal of their apocalyptic, might make it necessary for churchmen again to deal with revolutionary religion in their apologetic writings.

The Radical Testimony: The Spiritualizers

The spiritualizing tendency was a constant threat to the Free Church from the beginning, and influenced also the thinking of some persons who ultimately decided for the Church. Several of the personalities who led or contributed to revolutionary efforts subscribed to a doctrine of inspiration which, by itself, might have resulted in the destruction of community. But even the prophets Augustin Bader (?-1530) and David Joris (1501/2-1556) had their little bands of the faithful.[27] While Melchoir Hofmann (?-1543) gave major attention to the new gathering of the chosen people, the exodus of Israel from the midst of apostasy, the escape from the Egyptian corruption of the papacy, Bernt Rothmann (1495-1535) resolutely repudiated the doctrine of the Indwelling Word because it destroyed history and eschatology. If the atmosphere of such an age is utterly foreign to us, we should not assume that special revelation was a teaching limited to the marginal groups. Luther himself advised Philip of Hesse that before he acted like a patriarch he should attain their stature as stalwarts of God.[28] The reverse implication is clear, although in practice Luther hardly deviated from the scepticism he had expressed toward direct inward illumination in dealing in the early years with Stübner, Zwilling, and Storch, the "Zwickau prophets," (1521-22).

Among historians it was Alfred Hegler who first distinguished a clear line between the Anabaptists and the spiritualizers, establishing a distinction which Ernst Troeltsch popularized.[29] The spiritualizers were those whose spiritual and intellectual orientation made it impossible for them to accept the burden and offense of association with any earthly church. They had a vision of the Early Church, but this vision led them rather to despair of seeing a true Restitution. They hoped for a new Age, when it would be given to men to see the restored golden realm; this Age might be heralded by the appearance of a prophet with a special revelation and commission from God. But, unlike the chiliasts, they did not name the prophet's name; and they spent their years in "standing still" rather than identifying themselves with one of the "sectarian" communities. They looked for the time when "the Father of Mercy will give us the Key of David in our hearts, so that the closed Book, the secret of his will, will be opened"[30] but did not live to see it happen.

Like Hans Denck (c. 1495-1527), who drew up a list of contradictions in the Bible which only a direct gift of the Spirit could clarify,[31] they were puzzled by the signs of the times and were sure that all existing parties — Romans, Lutherans, Zwinglians, Anabaptists — read them incorrectly. The outward form of baptism was unimportant, for the true baptism is that of the soul. Faith is a free gift of God, and cannot be compelled either by the magistrates or by the exercise of the ban within the congregation.

Sebastian Franck (1499-1543) and Caspar Schwenckfeld (1489-1561), both of whom the Anabaptists were compelled eventually to exclude from their meetings, were perhaps the finest examples of this point of view. It was Franck who contributed the word *unpartheyisch* to the German language, a word which approximates to a remarkable degree what some of our twentieth-century contemporaries mean by "nonsectarian." The True Church, in this world of appearance and sham, could only exist as a hidden association of like spirits who might, indeed, be found among the Turks and heathen folk as readily as among those pretended Christians whose literalistic and mass-faith bore the marks of the Fall at the time of Constantine, or at the time of mass conversion of the Germanic tribes to the Roman standard. Although there were reported to be little groups of "Franckonists" in Holland into the second generation after him, it is evident that Franck's basic structure of thought is nonhistorical and moved even further away from the problems of the life of the Church.[32]

Caspar Schwenckfeld, who is still memoralized in a church bearing his name, was as nonhistorical as Franck in his system of thought — although more active in organizing little study and prayer groups for the understanding and practice of primitive Christianity. In *Von dem Kindertauf* he urged suspension of the rite; faith cannot be compelled, the Spirit goeth where it listeth (John 3:8). When, in 1545 or thereabout, Philip of Hesse asked him to write concerning his views on infant baptism he replied that he would rather not, for it was not important, an ordinance of man and not Scriptural; neither would he rebaptize.[33] A contemporary scholar has paid him the tribute:

> Yet it must appear characteristic that one of the greatest weaknesses of modern theology, especially in Protestantism, is the lack of productivity and originality in the thinking on the Holy Ghost. . . . In the crucial period of the Reformation, Schwenckfeld was aware of this embarrassment.[34]

Within the context of Christian history, however, this sounds very much like the oft-expressed regret that the genius of Montanism was lost to the Church. As a review of the long and extensive exchange between Schwenckfeld and Pilgram Marpeck (Strassburg, 1526-42) indicates, the centrifugal force of the spiritualizers' ideas was more than any continuing historical community could be expected to bear.

From the sixteenth century through Anne Hutchinson (1591-1643) and James Naylor (1618-80) to the present time there has been a continuing strain of prophetism and spiritualism in sectarian Protestantism. The Free Church never has been free from the spiritualizers' challenge in one form or another, and is not today. American religious history has been especially dotted by experiments in making concrete one or another form of special revelation. Oneida was such a colony, combining a "modern" and "scientific" approach to religion and society with Old Testament overtones. In the Mormon colonies of Nauvoo and the Great Salt Lake the Old Testament forms became more explicit. At Bethel and Aurora the life of the Church at Jerusalem (Acts 2, 4, and 5) was recapitulated. The Amana colonies, which became a joint stock company in 1936, attempted originally to organize government about a series of personalities imbued with the gift of the Spirit; unfortunately, the line ran out and no new prophet appeared to carry the tradition. In general, however, the threat to the integrity of the Church is much more evident today in various forms of the liberal gnosis; special revelation is again a particular fancy of the educated, or partly educated, rather than among the poor in spirit.

To be sure, Aimie Semple McPherson was a twentieth-century American phenomenon. But the special insights of Christian Science are perhaps more typical. Here again the appeal is made to a unique knowledge which unlocks the meaning of the universe, and in striking fashion combines the primitive Christian virtue of healing with the "scientific" world-view of idealistic philosophy. As a translator and professor of a tougher faith has summarized the situation:

> Although there are few philosophers nowadays who profess dependence upon Hegel, it is very apparent that his ideas live on in the Idealistic philosophies which were regnant only yesterday and which colored the Liberal Theologies which by reason of the notorious conservatism of religion, are influential even today. For a long while I puzzled over the fact that Christian Science, so called, acquired rapidly so many adherents who were drawn from various Protestant Churches, and more especially over the fact that these people were not in the least aware that they were exchanging their religion for one which was radically different, inasmuch as it has no personal God, looks back to no decisive historical Incarnation, knows no present Instant of rebirth, and looks forward to no conclusive day of judgment and

> resurrection. In the end I understood that they were quite right in thinking that they had in fact made no violent transition, but had only progressed farther in the direction they were already going, preferring naturally enough the consistent Idealism of Christian Science to the less thorough-going Idealism of modern Liberal Christianity, which is still hampered by historical factors, by traces of dualistic realism, and by other incongruous elements which are vestiges of the older tradition.[35]

This brings the issue back to where it really rests, to the widely prevalent spiritualizing tendencies *within* our churches today. It is increasingly evident that the widespread resistance to a historical revelation, the refusal to exercise the most elementary disciplines, the substitution of a set of petty moralisms for the glorious militancy of a people whose hope is in things to come, represent in our churches the most serious threat to a living faith. Sometimes this gnosis is presented in terms which remind one of Melchior Hofmann at Strassburg, as in the introduction to a little book of broad horizons recently published:

> As we listened to Dr. Booth there on our little island apart, we knew that this was our day of Pentecost. Tongues of fire descended upon us. These were words of a universal language. It was the voice of humanity, the passion of a Great Soul reaching out to all souls.[36]

That the Great Soul mentioned did not fail to proclaim an apparently new, but actually quite old, dispensation for all goodhearted people (Sebastian Franck's *"alle gutherzige Leute"!*) is clear in the inspired proclamation:

> Upon a universalized basis which admits the presence of the living God in non-Christian religions as well as in Christian; upon a basis of truth for which the teachings of science are the guide; upon the centrality of the Jesus of history in interpreting the purposes of God; upon the affirmation that God has new light for each succeeding stage of civilization — upon these the Coming Great Church must be built.

> Conscious of the multitude of gentle hearts, of quiet fearless spirits, of willing hands, and of keen intelligent minds, all of whom desire to love and to serve as this new and awakened humanity enters into the temple of the spiritual life, we need not fear the dissolution of all the churches of the present as we hail the Coming Great Church.
>
> Every religious faith of earth, not only our Protestant-Catholic Christianity, must find its home in the God our sons will worship. . . . I plead for a religion based upon the nature of piety in our human experience.[37]

It is the stock-in-trade of such people not only to depreciate the organized churches and repeat the old Joachimite myth of a New Age of the Spirit, but to attack the painful efforts of the churches in the ecumenical movement to reweave the seamless robe of Christ. Daniel Jenkins has correctly assessed the more determined elements, those who at least have paid history the tribute of fostering intentional communities:

> A third factor in the present theological situation, which also weakens the ecumenical movement, is the divorce between our modern "spiritualizers" and both the Catholic and the Protestant revivals. By the "spiritualizers" I mean those who exalt the Spirit over the Word and over tradition, and who, possessed by a passion for Christian perfection, go out and separate themselves from the world in little groups of their own. They have exercised a strong influence on many aspects of English religion ever since the time of the sectaries of the seventeenth century, to go back no farther, and their point of view finds powerful expression in the writings of Middleton Murry and in the activities of the very widespread community movement.[38]

This matter will be mentioned again in discussion of the peculiar dangers of the "American religion." For the present it is sufficient to emphasize that the spiritualizers are today, as they have been for four hundred years in almost unchanged form, a disintegrating and destructive factor of major importance to the Free Churches. It is all very well that Christianity is a "Spirit"; but, as the Anabaptists also knew, a spirit without a body is a ghost. And the individual "spirit" is by no means of necessity thrall to the Holy Spirit. The freedom which is worthy of a Christian man is that which is in Christ Jesus and his yoke. The real joy of a Christian man is not in unrestrained emancipation of self, but in confident hope in a Father who keeps His promises.

There is a future of splendor to be sure, but it is not an age when the Christian Church has withered away and all speak Esperanto and worship with Baha'i!

> In my opinion whatever we may have to go through now is less than nothing compared with the magnificent future God has planned for us. The whole creation is on tiptoe to see the wonderful sight of the sons of God coming into their own. The world of creation cannot as yet see Reality, not because it chooses to be blind, but because in God's purpose it has been so limited — yet it has been given hope. And the hope is that in the end the whole of created life will be rescued from the tyranny of change and decay, and have its share in the magnificent liberty which can only belong to the children of God![39]

The Radical Testimony: The Restitution of the True Church

Against the revolutionaries on the one hand, and the spiritualizers on the other, the Anabaptists set forth to realize in concrete form that life and order which they saw plainly expounded in the New Testament. Especially after their experience with various special revelations and with the principle of individual inspiration, they wanted to know nothing but the Bible *"interpretans non prophetans."* This was a visible, mobile and yet ordered, community — and not a matter of imagination.[40] Grebel wrote to his brother-in-law, the Swiss Reformer Vadian, in criticism of those Reformers who had not given the leadership for which they had hoped.

> Very learned shepherds and they that appear as pillars and leaders of the Word, as they in fact are, because of

> the fact that they drink of the purest water, yet do trample with their feet much water for the sheep and do drink first themselves in not a few places that still adhere firmly to the faith. You do not believe, I know, with what nettled feeling I hear of it, after having failed to restrain even the greatest leader of the Word, who asperses myself as a shop of envy and an angel of light and hypocrisy from Satan. That which happens here is happening also at Wittenberg; but the fair reader will judge from the booklets of Karlstadt how Luther goes backward and how outstanding he is as a trimmer and vigorous as a defender of his scandal.[41]

"The Scripture cannot be broken" (Thomas von Imbroich), and it gives a plain account of the manner in which the Lord expected His people to order their congregations. Laying the glosses aside, and the learned expositions of the professional theologians, the congregations should in both belief and order return to the simplest formulation and avoid speculation. The sermons and pastoral letters were frequently outlined on the Lord's Prayer, or the Apostles' Creed.

> For it is better and more certain to build on Christ and his teaching than to depend on fathers and councils. For Christ the Lord will be the Judge on that final day and not pope, fathers, councils.[42]

The True Church was a visible and disciplined Community, and not spiritualized in the individualistic sense; neither was it spiritualized in the Lutheran style, as "the invisible church." It was a covenantal community, with both the Key of David and the Keys of Peter.[43] It was based upon a certain view of the primitive Christian Church.

> As Luther distanced himself from the "Enthusiasts" and fought them, so Menno opposed a similar development within the Anabaptism of his homeland. Indeed his first writing dealt with this fight, in which he turned against the Münster kingdom — which was an outbreak of allegorical interpretation of the Bible and of chiliastic prophetism. He will not have his candor in appearance

> understood through a "Revelation or heavenly Inspiration," but only through the "plain, textual Word of the Lord." He doesn't want to know anything of "personal opinions, dreams and visions." In a defensive writing he cried out angrily that he was neither an Elijah nor an Enoch, neither a "third David" nor a visionary or Prophet.[44]

This was a "high" doctrine of the Church, and can be considered "sectarian" only if one accepts the territorial definition of the Church or exaggerates the importance of the spiritualizers in the Free Church tradition. In the Confession at Trieste (1539), as in Georg Zaunring's *Ain kurtze Annzaigung,* the Church is a living temple, the Body of Christ.[45] It is the means of salvation, the residence and realm of the Holy Spirit. When Leonhard Schiemer criticized Luther's translation of John 1:4, he made the point vividly. Luther had written, "the Word became flesh and dwelt among us." Schiemer said it was "*in* us, as all students know."

> Such is Luther's usage: he hopes on God, believes on Christ. We however believe not *on,* but *in* Christ. We have the Word *in* us and not *among* us.[46]

Lydia Mueller, like most historians and theologians who have since interpreted the Anabaptists' doctrines of the Church and the Holy Spirit, thought that Schiemer was defending the idea of individual inspiration; what moved him, as it has moved all true Free Churchmen, was *not inspiration but incarnation.* The Church was central, in its simple New Testament form:

> XVIII. They have no rulers, one is like the other, all equal in the service of one another.
>
> XX. When they are together it is their custom to speak of the Word of God and to admonish one another in brotherly fashion.[47]

This is the teaching about the nature of the Church, and about the work of the Holy Spirit, which both the legal establishments and the culturally established Free Churches have since neglected to their peril.

The connection of the destroyed Continental Anabaptist movement of the sixteenth century and the Free Churches of the seventeenth century in England has yet to be portrayed in detail, though the evidence is there. In any case, the Free Churchmen of the English tradition, too, have never admitted that their concern was anything less than the Church itself. The magistrates must keep aloof from the discipline of the Church because authority belongs properly to the Holy Spirit Himself. This was the original and authentic ground of religious liberty: not in the name of any general freedom, but a liberty reserved to the life of which the Holy Spirit was the Master and Christ the King. Nor was the conscience of the individual believer autonomous; the common prayer, study, and discussions, the brotherly admonition and exhortation were the touchstones against which his own leading was constantly to be referred. The magistrate must

> leave Christian religion free to every man's conscience, and . . . handle only civil transgressions, injustice, and wrongs of man against man, in murder, adultery, theft, etc., for Christ only is the King and Lawgiver of the Church and conscience.[48]

This was the conviction for which they were prepared to pay a high price: not that their freedom was restricted, but more positively that the True Church could be preserved and the Gospel spread abroad only where the magistrate kept out of matters which were not his proper concern.

For this high doctrine of the integrity of the Church many fled to Holland and America, and refused to return to submit regardless of the appeals made to their patriotism. For an England which persecuted those who obeyed the Bible belonged to the fallen condition of man, and was ruled by Anti-Christ himself.

> A seconde part of your letter is that you wold perswade vs to returne home into England, which you make no

Question wold be much pleasing to God, but we make great Question therof yea we hold it withowt all Question, the same should be much and highly displeasing vnto oure good God and father, that hath in his merciful providence brought vs owt of Babilon the mother of all abominations the habitation of devils and the holde, of all foule spirites and a cage of every vncleane and hateful birde.[49]

This was the mood of the radical Puritans contrasting with the moderate tones of the Presbyterian Reformers. Exile was also a witness to the Truth, and the simple forms of a covenant of families could be readily adapted to the most adverse circumstances. Thus at Salem, 1629, the faithful repeated the Covenant of Scrooby in the old country:

We convenant with the Lord and one with another; and do bynd ourselves in the presence of God, to walke together in all his waies, according as he is pleased to reveale himself unto us in his blessed word of truth.[50]

Here again is evidence of how far the later men of the Free Church were from any modern principle of individualism, or any ancient principle of individual inspiration. As John Robinson (1576?-1625) wrote an opponent in justification of this separation, the gathering of the people into a convenant was a very simple process:

And for the gathering of a Church M.B. I tell you, that in what place soever, by what means soever, whether by preaching the Gospell by a true Minister, by a false minister, by no minister, or by reading, conference, or any other means of publishing it, two or three faithful people do arise, separating themselves fro (m) the world into the fellowship of the gospell, and the covenant of Abraham, they are a Church truely gathered though never so weak, a house and temple of God rightly founded upon the doctrine of the Apostles and Prophets, Christ himsef (*sic*) being the corner stone, against which the gates of hell shall not prevayl, nor your disgracefull invectives neyther.[51]

There was undoubtedly a principle at work here which

could and did produce many diversions in Protestantism: but it was not the principle of individualism, as often claimed. Neither was it revolution. Neither was it a spiritualizing thrust. It was the same readiness to be guided by the Scriptures and by discussion aimed at a consensus by which the Anabaptists had been governed, by which Free Churches are governed, and which today is working also in many circles outside the Free Churches to bring all of the children of the Covenant back together again.

III. The Free Churches and Political Self-Government

Consensus

The Free Church congregations were not "self-governed" in the theological sense. They claimed to experience the governance of the Holy Spirit. Yet, in the sense that they rejected external political or ecclesiastical compulsions, and to the degree that they developed patterns of discussion and decision which could be extended to secular voluntary associations, they have made major contributions to the theory and practice of self-government. (Self-government as a term is generally to be preferred to "democracy" or "republicanism" in these times of slippery words.) Their presence should help to guarantee, moreover, that a society may not become too homogenized and centrally controlled in the development of its opinions — today no small matter.

The matters governed by consensus were many and various, and were limited only by appropriateness. That is, in the normal Free Church congregation, matters of apologetics, morals, ethics, organization, mission, and education all came under the guidance of the meeting. Of course the initial *fact* of faith was not subject to discussion: it was a presupposition of the meeting. In most cases, at least in the sixteenth century, the minimal agreement was stated in terms of the *Apostolicum Symbolum*. But even in those days it was in some cases a simple act of acceptance of the Covenant in Jesus Christ, and tacit agreement to take the Bible seriously. The acceptance of membership in a defined association, along with the accepting of the yoke of responsible membership in a purposeful group, was the prior condition for "talking up" a consensus on a given issue.

In the sixteenth century, with the exception of short-lived centers of refuge in Moravia and Poland, the Free Church pioneers had no opportunity to develop a positive contribution to society around them. To be sure, as Jakob Huter (c. 1536) assured the princes, their industry and sober behavior were qualities of benefit to any state. But generally speaking, Anabaptist doctrine was developed in a situation in which only two types of government were known: a) that which persecuted the Lord's people; and b) that which tolerated for the time, but might persecute on the morrow. The Anabaptists were continuously conscious of a truth which generally escaped the Lutheran and Calvinist writers until the time of persecution in Hitler's Germany: how near to the State of Romans 13 is the State of Revelation 13. With their long lists of martyrs, the books of martyrs' testimony, the hymns and letters celebrating those who sealed their testimony in knightly fashion with their blood, the Anabaptists developed no body of natural law. They could not assume any responsibility for the natural order. Living under savage persecution, and in an atmosphere heavily surcharged with expectation of the Last Things, they were concerned with their vocation as Christians rather than with a Christian definition of their vocations.

It was only in England and America that the Free Churches came to play a role in shaping the character of the state and society in which they lived. Here, in the comparative peace and stability eventually attained, they left an indelible stamp upon the development of Anglo-Saxon democracy. In politics as in religion, their first interest was the integrity of the Church, and the first premise of good government was that it made way for the living and proclaiming of the Truth of God.

> The motive behind their concern for the rights of the local congregation was not to safeguard an abstract individual liberty but to take seriously the fact of the Church as a community in its most concrete and immediate form.[1]

The derivative value to the society, however, was that

the principle of reaching a decision by discussion pointing to a consensus (informed discussion ⟶ consensus) was also carried into the secular realm both in theory and practice. The transfer of the "priesthood of all believers" to the political sphere is particularly marked in Cromwell, as his opposition to both the class principle of Ireton and the dogmatic formulae of the Levellers makes clear. Ireton would have restricted the suffrage to those holding a certain interest in a stable society by virtue of property ownership. The Levellers, on the other hand, were dogmatic egalitarians. But of Cromwell:

> For him the purpose of such machinery is to find something out, to discover something which is there to be discovered — discovered by hearing what each man's conscience has to say but also by frank and open discussion among men wishing to learn the will of God. What he has learned from his experience of the small democracy of the Christian congregation is the insight into the purposes of life which the common life and discussion of a democratic society can give as nothing else can.
>
> The root of the matter is that if the disussion is at all successful, we discover something from it which could have been discovered in no other way.[2]

The application of the principle of consensus, which in the life of the Anabaptists and their successors in the Church had been the channel through which the Holy Spirit made His will known to His people, was of revolutionary importance in the political sphere. It still is. Even today — or perhaps, with the rise of millennialist politics, we should say *especially* today — it is an imperative reminder of the "doubtfulness things are involved in" — and a reminder that a decision which represents the best wisdom available requires full and informed discussion on the part of all concerned. We are prone to become enraptured by the mechanics of parliamentary representation, and to forget that the counting of heads is simply a technique for attempting to arrive at "the sense of the meeting." Each is prone to assert his individual freedom, and forget that consensus can be attained only by the active and responsible participation of even "the poorest he." Parliamentarianism has become in some countries the disease of democracy, the very denial of effective self-government.

We are particularly adept today in reaching quick and dogmatic formulations of past experience — "the will of the majority," "absolute separation of church and state," "academic freedom," "women's rights" — and forget that the genius of our free institutions, so far as the Free Churches contributed to them, is precisely the willingness to carry through a continuing discussion with those who do not presently agree with us. One need only contrast the thinking in the decisions of *Everson* v. *Board of Education* (1947), *McCollum* v. *Board of Education* (1948), and *Zorach* v. *Clauson* (1952) to see the difficulties caused by "political fundamentalism" on the one hand and loose thinking on the other. True liberty, in the political and the religious sense, is neither libertinism in a state of anarchy nor is it servility in a People's Democracy;[3] it is based on a continuing discussion which leads to a solution avoiding the opposite perils of rigid secularism and establishment. When a democracy is successful, "it is a common life, a real community in which men's differences supplement instead of thwarting one another" (A. D. Lindsay).

The existence of Free Churches, along with other free and voluntary associations in a body politic, is in itself a guarantee of full discussion at the subpolitical level during the preparation which precedes political decisions which are informed and adequate.

> The corollary of that is Lord Acton's doctrine that liberty is possibly only in a society where there are centres of organization other than the political. Nothing so much makes possible a public opinion which is real because it is based on free and frank discussion as the existence of independent voluntary organizations with public purposes.[4]

As we shall see, it is a basic strategy on the part of totalitarian

regimes, both Nazi and Communist, to destroy all such i
pendent centers of finance, organization, and opinion.
sham "democracy," which is simply the voice of the peo
at a given moment (the mob) is one thing; a democra
which is a healthy pattern of discussion aimed at reaching
genuine consensus is quite another.

As can readily be seen, the charge that democracy e
thrones the principle of individualism is patently fals
Neither is democracy opposed to discipline; the basic que
tion is *how* the discipline is to be reached — i.e., whether it
is dictated or "talked up." Leadership itself, and its style, is plainly different in kind when it has been selected and conditioned by previous levels of debate and discussion. Adolph Loewe has pointed up the matter, in so far as English political and social history is concerned:

> . . . it would be a misinterpretation of the facts if we were to equate English liberalism with an atomistic structure of society. What strikes the observer of this period of English history who compares England with the great continental nation, is not extreme individualism, but the general tendency to form voluntary associations. From the political parties down to the chapel meetings, public life was actually dominated by self-governing bodies, growing up spontaneously but submitting to the principle of democratic leadership.[6]

The foundations for the pattern of voluntarism which became so marked by the nineteenth century had been laid in the seventeenth, and in this groundwork of English democracy the Free Churches played no small role. The final effect, in the political field, is finely demonstrated by the operation of the House of Commons. When the Parliament building was rebuilt after the recent war, the room where the Commons meet was deliberately kept small, with seats for only about two-thirds of the membership. In all but the most unusual sessions the members sit close together in a meeting which is both physically and atmospherically a town meeting. As Edmund Burke explained it to the Sheriffs of Bristol, they meet not as delegates defending

al areas and interests but to discuss and decide for the
le. That is to say, at its best the House of Commons
ike a congregational meeting.

ligious Liberty, the Negative Phase: Separation of Church and State

The most direct contribution of the Free Churches to
idual citizen, whether church member or not, was
hment of liberty of conscience. It is important
we mean by religious liberty.
the asserted right of an estab-
in peonage in two-thirds of all
Does "religious liberty" cover
ablished church to a compulsory
on of children? Does "religious
ty" demands of the Greek Orthodox
urch to a monopoly on the sale of wax candles through-
ut that nation, and for an exemption of the Attica area
arm lands from resettlement of landless farmers? Is it an infringement of "religious liberty" when an anti-clerical government finally breaks one of these churchly cartels, and opens a field to free competition by various voluntary religious bodies? The questions are not rhetorical; such charges are made daily. On another front we have the statement of Professor Emil Fuchs of Leipzig at a recent "Peace Day" in Weimar: "Since the Reformation the Churches have never been so free as today in the Soviet Zone."[7] It is apparently worthwhile to refer again to the classics and history of the struggle for religious liberty.

According to William Penn, in 1687:

> I ever understand an impartial liberty of conscience to be the natural right of all men, and that he that had a religion without it, his religion was none of his own. For what is not the religion of a man's choice is the religion of him that imposes it: so that liberty of conscience is the first step to have a religion.[8]

In the background we see the memory of persecutions, and

the determination to achieve a right relation in the life of the True Church. In 1946, the Archbishop of York defined religious liberty in the House of Lords:

> Freedom to worship according to the conscience and to bring up children in the faith of their parents; freedom for the individual to change his religion; freedom to preach, educate, publish and carry on missionary activity; and freedom to organize with others and to acquire and hold property for those purposes.[9]

This reflects the mood of an institution which has long enjoyed freedom from political suppression or intervention, and which yet enjoys patronage. It is framed largely in individualistic terms. The Charter of the United Nations has an article on religious freedom, as follows:

> Article 18: Everyone shall have the right to freedom of thought, conscience and religion. This right shall include freedom to maintain or to change his religion or belief, and freedom either individually or collectively and in public or private, to manifest his religion or belief in worship, observance, practice and teaching.[10]

Passing by the fact that in Spain, Italy, Colombia, China, Poland, Russia, among others, even the above form of words is violated, it is worth noting that this statement is faulty on two fronts and reveals the common misunderstanding of religion as an individualistic prerogative. As such it has wandered rather far from the classical Free Church position, and the faith of the pioneers of religious liberty. A church which is truly free has not only the function of assembling individuals who have the right freedom to exercise their personal beliefs; it has as *Church* the duty to maintain discipline and to carry a mission: i.e., to proclaim its Truth in the open forum of truth. Secondly, the right and duty of a church to be the Church — to be in its situation representative in the fullest sense of the Church Universal — is in no sense dependent upon a benevolent grant from government or governments. The true status of the Church *chronologically* precedes the first prerogative of any contemporary sovereign power, and in a free society it is bound up with those historic rights which *logically* antecede the frame of government itself.

Religious liberty is a historical achievement, not primarily a speculative abstraction, and it is best defined *negatively* in terms of the historic struggle against suppression and persecution, and *positively* in terms of the discipline and mobility which characterize the Free Churches when they are true to their principles. *And the positive factor is prior to the negative, both historically and logically.* A church which is truly a temple of Christian Liberty, in short, is a community of Biblical faith governed by the Holy Spirit and by no other power or influence. And a church which has embraced some new dispensation, or has abandoned Christian discipline for the easy path of the spiritualizers of culture-religion is not a Free Church, however bravely it may boast of its independence of political controls. In another chapter we shall consider whether, and to what extent, the churches in America are today Free Churches in the proper sense of the term.

The American Experiment: Liberty, not Toleration

Before discussing contemporary problems posed by the "American religion," further reference to the historic role of the Free Churches in the formative period of the American Republic will help to illuminate the contributions of these churches to a free society.[11]

The American system is different from that set up first at Westphalia (1648), repeated in the time of the Toleration Act in Britain (1690), in which the government supports one or more religions and permits others to exist relatively undisturbed.[12] It is different from any Roman Catholic teaching, the most liberal of which can only concede the value of liberty if itself a minority, or grant toleration if suppression will not succeed. It is different in kind from the Protestantism of Europe, which also produced establishments here in America during the colonial period. These colonial "state churches," which were perpetuated in some measure until 1819 in Connecticut and until 1833 in Massachusetts, resulted in all of the familiar problems: internal latitudinarianism, rending of society by persecution and forced emigration, abridgement of related liberties of citizens. The American system, as it came to be expressed in the provisions of the Virginia Bill of Rights (1778), represented the triumph of Free Church principles in the New World.

Rufus Jones once expressed a judgment on this point, which is shared by William Warren Sweet and other historians of American Christianity:

> If it had not been for the disorders into which some of the Anabaptist leaders fell, and the fanaticism which possessed the minds of some of their leaders particularly after they were harried to desperation by persecution, and above all, if it had not been for the wild outbursts of insanity at Münster, the democratic idea of church control and management would no doubt have made its way more effectively, and would have won great place in the thought of that age. Even as it was, in spite of all the handicaps, Anabaptism proved to be one of the most virile and contagious of all the new religious ideals of the reforming epoch. But after the events of Münster in 1534, the name Anabaptism produced a shudder of horror in every conservative-minded person, as, once again, Bolshevism has done in our time, and from the date of Münster no one consciously adopted ideas and principles which owed their origin to that opprobrious movement.
>
> And yet, as has happened many times before and since, with movements that have been showered with scorn and opprobrium, the conquered and defeated became in the end the conqueror . . . when nearly every one of the constructive principles of the Anabaptists got written into the Constitution of the United States, or got expressed in some important branch of American Christianity.[43]

Although Rufus Jones' writings are not too reliable as to the connection of the Anabaptists with other groups in the "Left

Wing of the Reformation,"[14] his statement that the "conquered and defeated became in the end the conqueror" is itself a favorite notion of the radicals and his general appraisal of what happened in America is a true one.

We should be quite clear, as many people today are not, that *religious liberty* and *toleration* are quite different concepts — although to the private citizen they may feel much the same. As the political authority of the Church has declined, in modern times, the Church of England, the Church of Sweden, the Church of Württemberg, and others have found it expedient to yield many of their old prerogatives. In the breaking up of Christendom, the Constantinian pattern of coercion eventually became unworkable. Thus, the British High Court interpreted the Toleration Act of 1688:

> It is now no crime . . . for man to say that he is a dissenter; nor is it any crime for him not to take the sacrament according to the rites of the Church of England; nay, the crime is if he does it, contrary to the dictates of his conscience. . . . The Toleration Act renders that which was illegal before now legal; the dissenter's way of worship is permitted and allowed by this Act.[15]

But this is a pragmatic solution, and the implication of generous restraint by a government with the right to act in religious matters cannot escape democratic criticism. As Friedrich Hecker of Baden once summed it up (quoting Paine): "Toleration is not the opposite of Intolerance, but its counterfeit. Both are Despotism."[16] The authority still rests with a governmental act to determine when, where, and to what extent, dissent is allowed. A genuine bill of rights, on the contrary, sets a boundary beyond which no power of government properly may go; it is not just a declaration of liberality and good intention which is in the final analysis not binding on Parliament or Deputies.[17]

Nor is religious liberty to be confused with a pluralistic establishment. Here the experience of the state of Virginia in achieving religious liberty is instructive. After independence, many good men believed that it was still essential to use religion to undergird the commonwealth: George Washington and Patrick Henry proposed that the government collect church taxes and apportion them according to the number of members listed for the various denominations. In a great political battle the opposition party, led by James Madison, won out. Madison and his friends knew, of course, that it is common practice for establishments to list as "members" large numbers who are not really members at all — thereby producing a disproportion in the division of church taxes. But, more fundamentally, they believed that government has no proper authority in religious affairs, neither to persecute nor to tolerate, nor even to support. The bill reads:

> No man shall be compelled to frequent or support any religious worship, place or ministry, whatsoever, nor shall suffer on account of his religious opinions or belief; opinion in matters of religion shall in no wise diminish, enlarge, or affect civil capacities. The rights hereby asserted are of the natural rights of mankind.[18]

The Virginia stand was recapitulated, with slight modification, in the federal Constitution.

When the federal Constitution was sent to the states for ratification (1789-91) it became apparent that many had been expecting a bill of rights along with it. Perhaps Thomas Jefferson, writing from Paris, expressed the popular sentiment:

> I wish with all my soul that nine first conventions may accept the new Constitution, to secure us the good it contains; but I equally wish that the four latest, whichever they may be, may refuse to accede to it till a declaration of rights be annexed.[19]

Something very like that happened; at least in North Carolina ratification was first refused, on the basis that certain inalienable rights had to be secured prior to the compact.[20] The provision finally made forbade the government to legislate "respecting an establishment of religion, or prohibiting the free exercise thereof."

The parallelism of the contract which initiated the state and national frames of government with the Covenants which bound the Free Churches was remarkable. At the first of the constitutional conventions held to provide government following separation from England, a meeting of New Hampshire towns proclaimed:

> It is our humble opinion that when the Declaration of Independence took place, the Colonies were absolutely in a state of nature, and the powers of government reverted to the people at large.[21]

During the fifteen years which saw the English throne replaced by representative forms of government within each colony and nationally, congregations heard many sermons on the text, II Samuel 5:3.

> So all the elders of Israel came to the King at Hebron: and David made a covenant with them in Hebron before the Lord: and they elected David King over Israel.

In American tradition, the religious covenant precedes the political covenant: in the former they are gathered together as bondsmen of Christ in a common life; in the latter, they establish order and simultaneously secure their inalienable liberties. The classical American doctrine of the political compact has as little to do with the romantic idea of the state as has the democratic fellowship of a Free Church with the carefully codified power structure of an establishment. The Free Churches and representative government are complementary to each other. Each, in its own way, is a situation in which the members concerned (in one case, the baptized; in the other, all members of the citizenry) are governed by the continuing effort to reach a consensus as to what the Will of God may be in a given moment of decision.

Danger Signs: Three Cases

It is fairly evident that we do not, either as churchmen or citizens, always attain the perfection to which such a standard calls us. There have been at least three interesting type cases recently in which instruments of government in America have presumed to restrain the intention of the churches to be guided by a Higher Power: 1) in delaying the planned union of the Evangelical and Reformed Church with the Congregational and Christian Churches; 2) in the case of Andrew Yoder, disciplined by the bishops of the Amish for breaking the terms of his church membership;[22] and 3) in the Melish case in a parish of the Protestant Episcopal Church in New York City. In the first instance a judge in a federal court saw fit to expound at length on the history and doctrine of the Congregational Churches to the best scholars of that connection. In the second, the farm of a church leader was sold by court order to pay an uncontested fine, because with other responsible officials he had exercised a Free Church discipline over three hundred years old: the ban.[23] One who doubts that proper exercise of Matthew 18:15-17 involves shunning as well as expulsion may nevertheless be disturbed that civil government should enter the picture.

In the Melish case, where the United States Supreme Court finally refused to overrule an ouster injunction issued and confirmed by New York state courts, some three thousand Protestant ministers signed a protest against civil court intervention in an ecclesiastical case as constituting

> . . . an unwarranted intrusion of the civil power of the state in a religious controversy in violation of the Constitutional separation of Church and State.[24]

(Mr. Melish has in the meantime apparently put himself in defiance of church law, and civil court action may yet be necessary and justifiable.) As Umphrey Lee has shown in a study of the problem, there is in America a widespread notion of general social control taking priority over the natural rights of individuals and associations.[25] If "culture religion" continues to find rootage in our soil, the power of government as a standardizing agency in the moral and religious field will be correspondingly enhanced.

Danger Zone: The Public School and the Church

In no area is our present confusion more evident than in the field of education.[26] In the earlier years of American society no one, whatever his doctrine of the Church, doubted that true education implied a certain fund of religious knowledge. Such knowledge was to be as nonsectarian as possible, and did not commonly involve the special doctrines or rites of individual churches. Of the value of bringing to succeeding generations knowledge of the Bible and of general truths no one, from George Washington to Thomas Jefferson, was in doubt. When Thomas Bray, at the turn of the eighteenth century, was soliciting monies for schools he stressed the importance of theology:

> In the first place, this is a Knowledge Conversant about the greatest Objects, God, and our selves; *Secondly,* and that about the grandest and most Concerning Truths relating to those Objects. *Thirdly,* It is a Knowledge to which the most considerable of other Sciences are some way or other appendant and subservient. *Fourthly,* It is A Knowledge founded upon more certain Principles than all other Sciences whatsoever (scarce the Mathematicks excepted) All which speak the Noble Nature of Divine Knowledge. And Lastly, It is the only knowledge which can conduct us safe through the Mazes and Labyrinths of this World, to our Rest and Happiness in the other; Which does eminently shew the Usefulness of it.[27]

This is also part of the American tradition, although some of the presuppositions on which Bray's attitude rested are today strange to a large part of the American people.

The public school movement, which began to come into is own just a hundred years ago, was intended in America to make educational opportunities more general, not to secularize education. Today, among the various social institutions which condition and control the local community, and determine the direction of the next generation, the public school has become dominant. In a healthy situation the young personality is shaped up in a friendly co-operation of several agencies: the family, the church, the school, the voluntary civic clubs. In recent years in America the school has pressed to the fore, and with the growth of educational lobbies and teachers' unions the control has well-nigh left the local community and its families. Primary education has made real strides in methodology; unfortunately, it has become dominated to a marked degree by a philosophy of social positivism which is at odds with Biblical understandings of man and his destiny. No more serious challenge confronts the faith at home than the secularized school, which is quite different from the public school independent of sectarian control.

A colleague of the author's at the University of Michigan had the following representative experience. It was during the season when everyone was discussing Thomas Mann's epic, *Joseph in Egypt.* The school class attended by my colleague's daughter was to put on a little play, "The Story of Joseph." As she studied her mimeographed manuscript, prepared by the teacher, one evening at home, she suddenly turned to her father. The manuscript put in Joseph's mouth in that tragi-comic moment when Joseph "fled leaving his shirt": "Oh no! Potiphar might not like it!" Said the little girl, some memory of Bible reading arousing doubts, "Did Joseph really say *that,* Daddy?" And her father answered: "No, my dear. He said, 'How can I do this great wickedness, and sin against God?' " The incident is revealing. It shows the specific consequences of a philosophy of education where "Moses is Nobody,"[28] and God is an anachronism. Because the old sanctions of morality seemed irrelevant, the modern teacher felt free to rewrite Joseph's virtue in terms of prudential considerations. What happens in an age when Potiphar simply doesn't care is the quandary which confronts every "cut-flower" civilization — to use Elton Trueblood's excellent phrase. This *is* the age in which old sanctions and religious premises are abandoned; and all the appeals for a heightened morality, in the name of our nation's well-being and the future of democracy, will neither artificially nor prudently reconstruct a pattern of life which ultimately rests on faith in God and his Righteousness, a faith which the irresponsibles have so frivolously sought to tear down.

Moreover, the German experience with National Socialism gives clear evidence as to the dangers of putting education into the hands of methodological experts with a third-rate philosophy. Werner Richter has summarized this record quite conclusively in his book, *Re-educating Germany*. In the pre-Hitler period education of children fell from the hands of the cultured and truly educated, into the hands of the "non-commissioned officers" of primary education. These "non-coms" were the educational technicians, who had been held back from the universities and required to take a special training in which they saw from afar the benefits of cultural education but were not disciplined by them.

> . . . the elementary school teacher was to be discouraged from seeking a really fruitful academic preparation; hence his training had to be different from the rest of the teaching profession.[29]

He was cut off from the lot of the professors and even secondary school teachers, and he became willy-nilly a politician. Many became ministers of education and others occupied high posts in the Nazi movement, of which the teachers were among the most fanatical supporting groups. Nowhere in history can be seen more clearly the danger of entrusting power over youth to the inchoate longings, the frustrated ambitions, the half-coherent social philosophy, of an element but semi-cultured and very modestly exposed to the intellectual disciplines.

We are not so far along in the American scene. Yet it is plainly evident that our public schools have fallen into the hands of the technicians from the trade schools, that the academic requirements set for public school teachers are long on methods and short on cultural subjects, that the educational departments and associations have the role also of political lobbies. Especially symbolic is the fact that the best educated and most cultured persons in our community are commonly prevented by law from participating in the education of our younger children.[30] These are real problems, which cannot be answered by dogmatic cliches about the "separation of church and state" or other slogans.

A proper discontent with teachers' colleges and schools of education has come to characterize many concerned parents and churchmen who are not in sympathy with the more violent attacks being made on the public schools from some quarters. And it is only accurate to say that this discontent will continue to grow until fairly met and answered; the answer will involve a rediscovery of the proper service of the school to the family and the church, in its auxiliary role as transmitter of culture and stimulus to the love of sound learning among our youth.

> Those who have the most influence in public education in this country — the professors in the schools of education, the administrators, and pressure groups like the National Education Association — have built up in the past twenty or thirty years a rigid body of doctrine which has been erected into an official gospel. As the end results of this gospel are gradually revealed, many people who believe in and want to further good public education are finding these results less than satisfactory — and they are saying so, out loud. For educators to lump all these people together as reactionaries, even by implication, is unjust, and might be an indication of panic on the part of the educators. Let them stop name-calling, and meet sincere criticism on the level of honest intellectual discussion.[31]

It is a Protestant as well as a Roman Catholic conviction that "Responsibility for the children is not an issue between parents and educational administrators, but between the parents and God."[32]

Yet our Free Churches in America often have shown themselves not at all clear as to the issues involved. Such a journal as *The Christian Century,* which might be taken to represent an influential body of American Protestant opinion, has been so negatively influenced by the "Roman Catholic threat" as to write of the "duty of the State to educate." Writing of a recent controversy on taxing of private church schools in California, one of its editors expresses the opinion,

> The California contest is of national interest because it brings the church-state issue to focus on the tax question. So long as the states retain their rights under the Constitution, California is entitled to tax parochial schools whether other states exempt them or not. It is free to reject the claim, as it has done for a century, that parochial schools serve the public interest in education as well as do the public schools. And it is free to assert that when nonpublic purposes are served by such schools they must acknowledge their essential character by payment of tax.[33]

Father John E. Wise has put forward a Roman Catholic position in the matter, in challenging irreligion as he sees it:

> . . . the fact that state schools teach a separation of religion and education . . . is not any more American than is the union of religion and education. The union of religion and education does not mean the union of church and state.[34]

There are other citizens besides Roman Catholics who are not content with an enforced secularism. And the answer is not to be found through a dogmatic assertion of speculative absolutes, particularly those of doubtful historical foundation. The answer or answers can only be found — and here should be the real contribution of those true to the Free Church tradition — in talking the matter up, in approaching the matter with a fresh spirit of inquiry in discussion, in striving to reach a consensus which will reflect the best wisdom available to us.

The matter of religious liberty, like our other rights as citizens, is a specific historical phenomenon and not an abstract proposition. It refers to immediate relationships, some of which have been satisfactorily defined in the past, and some of which are subject to re-examination in the light of present knowledge. It is not correctly understood purely in the negative sense of freedom from persecution. Certainly it does not imply a positive secularism in political instruments and public institutions. For the Free Church which is worthy of its calling the first question will always be how the Lord's will may best be done.

Voluntaryism

A third major contribution of Free Churches to the body politic, along with the method of reaching a consensus and the championing of our basic liberties, is in the gathering of voluntary communities of discipline and responsibility.[35] These voluntary associations parallel others in trade, professions, education, agriculture, labor. In leading into this positive aspect of religious liberty, the definition offered by Charles F. James is superior to others previously cited:

> By religious freedom, or soul liberty, is meant the natural and inalienable right of every soul to worship God according to the dictates of his own conscience, and to be unmolested in the exercise of that right, so long, at least, as he does not infringe on the rights of others; that religion is, and must be, a voluntary service; that only such service is acceptable to God; and, hence, that no earthly power, whether civil or ecclesiastical, has any right to compel conformity to any creed or any species of worship, or to tax a man for its support.[36]

Politically speaking, the principle of voluntaryism is the positive side of opposition to state interference in affairs of the Church. The contribution of the Free Churches has been not only in spreading the principle of voluntaryism abroad in an open society characterized by a wide variety of free institutions, but in developing certain patterns of internal health from which that society derives direct benefit.

One contribution of a vigorous faith may be indirect: in the higher morals and ethics resulting from a powerful religious movement. When Sidney Webb, no particular champion of the churches, made his sociological study of the English mining industry, he was brought to the conclusion:

> What is needed is the power of the Spirit that calls to a

> higher, more social, and more genuinely civilized life, the power which a hundred years ago was evoked by the religious revival of that time. Who shall today evoke a like spirit among the Durham miners?[37]

The particular strength of the Free Churches' contribution has been, however, not only in the indirect consequences of religious concern, but in the direct impact of communities of discipline whose life testifies that a better way is possible on a given issue.

An Example: "Talking up" the Anti-Slavery Witness

Take the witness of the Society of Friends in the matter of slaveholding. It took generations, from the time when a group of Germantown Mennonites and Quakers considered the anti-slavery appeal of George Keith (1693) to the time when the Providence meeting expelled Stephen Hopkins for refusing to release two slaves (1774), until this concern became a matter of discipline within the fellowship. But the concern was laid on the conscience of every generation, and lying back of it was the determination to attain ultimately a consensus on the matter.

The context in which the burden of slavery was "talked up" is plain from the beginning. In Keith's pamphlet:

> Therefore, in true *Christian Love,* we earnestly recommend it to all our friends and Brethren, Not to buy any Negroes, unless it were on purpose to set them free, and that such who have bought any, and have them at present, after some reasonable time of moderate Service they have had of them, or may have of them, that may reasonably answer to the Charge of what they have laid out, especially in keeping Negroes Children born in their House, when under Age, that after a reasonable time of service to answer that Charge, they may set them at Liberty, and during the time they have them, to teach them to read, and give them a Christian Education.[38]

By the time of John Woolman the issue had become more burning and burdensome. At the Philadelphia Yearly Meeting in 1758 he brought it to a decisive issue:

> Should we now be sensible of what He requires of us, and through a respect to the private interest of some persons, or through a regard to some friendships which do not stand upon an immutable foundation, neglect to do our duty in firmness and constancy, still waiting for some extraordinary means to bring about their deliverance, God may by terrible things in righteousness answer us in this manner.[39]

It took decades for the conscience of the societies to become "sensible" of what the Lord required and to set their own houses in order; there were many who did not understand the issue at first. Over decades their number decreased. Once they had attained a consensus ("sense of the meeting") within their own ranks and made it a matter of discipline, the Friends were prepared to declare throughout the whole of the Republic that slaves should be let free. There are many such issues in the history of the Free Churches, and not a few today, which need to be met not with simple moralisms and pious resolutions but with "the sword of the Spirit which is the Word of God" (Eph. 6:17).

A Current Problem Area: The Integrity of the Family

On some matters, clear general legislation may not be presently possible or desirable, although devoted Christian people can attain an internal ethic which is better than the minimum legal requirement. Consider the breakdown of the family in contemporary society. According to an eminent sociologist,

> That the family of the immediate future will move further toward atomism (promoting individualism in leaders and intellectuals, but liable to degenerate into atomism), seems highly probable. Except for the Christian Church — which is not popular among the directive forces of western society — no agency or group of persons seems fundamentally interested in doing anything other than facilitate this increasing atomism.[40]

The Free Churches traditionally have been aware that the

proper balance to individual liberty in the political sphere is true obedience within the Church; whatever the legal maximum on multiple marriages in an age which confuses "freedom" and "liberty," there is a minor minimum for those who live in the world of the Bible and under the direction of the Holy Spirit. It is of more than sociological importance that an intimate relation exists between mixed religious faiths and broken homes. When the percentages on divorce are broken down by confession, they show:

4.6% of Jewish marriages;
6.4% of Roman Catholic;
6.8% of Protestant;
15.2% of mixed marriages;
16.7% of marriages where neither belongs to a religious community.[41]

Although, as we shall see later, the discipline of the churches is no longer as coherent as one might wish, it is evident from these figures that the momentum of past conviction combines with present covert pressure of opinion within the congregations, to strengthen family stability.

The Duty of Free Churchmen to Participate Politically

The point here being made is not, it is realized, particularly congenial to some conservative Protestant congregations which have studied to maintain the nonpolitical outlook that characterizes the New Testament and was a mark of the persecuted Anabaptists. Furthermore, the conscriptive aspect of modern society's organization for violence, both external and internal,[42] has created in certain definite respects a more acute problem for Christians than existed during earlier periods when there were still geographical frontiers available for refuge. On the other hand, one does not have to periodize modern history by that glorious conjunction of the Protestant Reformation and the discovery of America, and join with Cotton Mather in a new salute to the *evangelium aeternum,*[43] to say that to the extent that the American democracy has adopted the principle of consensus as a guide to reaching decisions in policy it is different in kind from either persecuting or tolerating governments. America does represent something new and precious in human political history. A citizen who by the very fact of his presence participates in government, i.e., is himself a "magistrate," is in a position different from anything the Anabaptists of the sixteenth century or tolerated subjects of any other age could have conceived or understood. Some positive contributions to the health of our democracy are made even by the most aloof of religious communities. Is it not clear that at all points where the discussion is still open, where policy has not as yet crystallized, every Christian citizen should share his insights and lay the burden of his concerns before his neighbors? Is it not clear that the difference between attaining consensus in the congregation and in the town meeting is a difference in setting rather than a difference in kind?

IV. The Free Church vs. the "American Religion"

Religious Liberty, the Positive Phase: Democratic Discipline

The positive side of religious liberty which — when the separation of church and state is taken as the sole key — is often neglected, is more important than the negative phase. In the Anabaptist and later periods of Free Church history the prior concern was always true obedience to the Lord of the Church. Although the doctrine of the natural rights of the citizen in the political sphere is complementary to the view of the Church, in the Christian life itself the member has another concern than "freedom." It is unjust to the Reformers to ascribe to them the principle of individualism, and it is a fundamental error of interpretation to write, as has one scholar:

> The term "free church" has the double meaning of freedom from secular influence (e.g., from the side of the state) and of freedom from coercion in religious matters (e.g., compulsory discipline).[1]

The early Free Churchmen did not favor internal freedom in the Church. Every member was not only free but obligated to participate in the "talking up" of discipline; and the discipline itself was binding.

The sixteenth- and seventeenth-century criticism of the territorial churches was precisely that the establishments raised up no more Biblical order. The political magistrates were to be held back from the congregations not because they were intrinsically evil (the Anabaptists were not Cathari), but because governance in the Church belonged to the Holy Spirit. The Christian life is dedicated not to worship of a speculative Freedom, but to obedience to the God who governs. The Christian is today loyal to the free society because in that framework alone can man be truly Man as God intended him, and because it is most favorable to the mission of the Blessed Community. The Christian life stands under the yoke of Jesus Christ (Matt. 11:28-30). He only is perfectly free who is a bondsman to Christ. Blessed are the "harnessed."[2]

The implications of a positive principle of voluntaryism ("voluntary" in the legal sense, not in the theological) are many. For long conditioned to acceptance of the coercive pattern, even Christian theologians have been slow to work out the implications of the new situation. Yet it is of revolutionary significance in the whole history of religions.

> A new type of grouping appears which, though current throughout the history of civilization, has not always been adequately recognized. The feeling of solidarity developing in these new units is to a certain extent revolutionary. . . . This new form of grouping is characterized by the concept of relationship as spiritual fatherhood and spiritual brotherhood.[3]

It is an equally marked departure from the last fifteen hundred years of Christian history.

> The three typical types of classical Protestantism, Luther, Calvin and Cranmer, carried over into Protestantism a set of ideas that today in North America we regard as medieval. They believed for example that membership in the Christian Church is something into which a child is born — on the contrary, we believe today that membership in the Christian Church is the result of a self-conscious act of decision whereby on approaching maturity the Christian elects to join a voluntary and exclusive fellowship.[4]

Corpus Christi is a concept fitted to our classical American pattern, rather than *Corpus Christianum*. Yet in what American seminary is ten percent of the time given to study and analysis of the Free Church traditions that is customarily spent on the doctrines of Luther and Calvin? Moreover, there are other ways in which churches can become "established" besides the legal, and when we set the present relation of American churches to our culture against the classical Free Church testimonies the painful question arises: To what degree are the American churches "free," and in what direction?

Danger: Relativists and Spiritualizers

The original American pattern of disciplined and missionary Christian communities, enjoying the benevolent neutrality of governments which were themselves prepared to learn the Will of God, on occasion contrasts rather strongly with our present way of doing things. And, in spite of the tendency of church people to believe that the deterioration has all occurred on one side (i.e., the political), the facts are otherwise. True, it was dismaying to read the dictum of the Chief Justice of the Supreme Court a few years ago, to the effect that "nothing is more certain in modern society than the principle that there are no absolutes." From such relativism in the most highly placed custodian of our national heritage to the murder of Charles Binaggio on the streets of Kansas City was several hundred miles on the map; but a straight line connects the two points.

> The soul of this generation is like Noah's raven, which went forth, to and fro and found rest nowhere, because the earth was still covered with water, as in the beginning when creation began.[5]

But it is much more dismaying to read such statements as the following from "professors of theology" in two American institutions entrusted with training young men for the ministry:

> Religion, at its highest and best, is the devotion of the total self, through search, service and adoration, to the highest cause of which one is now conscious, providing that cause is deemed worthy of the devotion of all men, and is symbolic of ever higher unexplored values.[6]

The second:

> Complete adjustment in all conceivable ways between a person and his environment would eliminate both natural evil and ethical sin. . . . Science will lead us eventually to such a mastery of physical law that there will be but a minimum of natural evil. What a glorious record is being built in this field! The control of the laws of mother earth is such that all her sons eventually shall live in harmony with her. Sin in all its aspects is the result of the maladjustment of a sensitive organism to its environment.[7]

Such spiritualizing statements, as will be seen, fit very neatly into the patterns of thought of National Socialism and culture religion generally.[8] They cut the nerve of the true Free Church testimony, with its emphasis upon discipline and mobility.[9] When taken seriously in the churches, they provide no adequate ground for suffering under persecution, for outlasting tyranny, or toward helping to maintain that creative tension between subpolitical communities of opinion which is so important to the open society. Such doctrine is sub-Christian in theology and pretotalitarian in politics.

The True Church: Disciplined and Mobile

A religious association or individual that has cordially embraced the spirit of the times, that has settled either intellectually or practically into external culture patterns which in fact dictate the life relationships, has abandoned the path of the pilgrim people of whom the Bible speaks and which Anabaptist history records. A concept of mobility was from the beginning basic to the Free Churches. The faithful must be gathered up; they must be prepared at any time to wander. The direct application of the Great Commission (Mark 16, Matthew 28) to every believing person, an interpretation which the Reformers commonly denied, was brought to bear. The True Church was, therefore, in tension with the culture in which it found itself at any period. Between the Christian community and the natural society was a borderline, a cutting edge of Christian discipline, the fence between the Lord's flock and the world at large. A plain-spoken message about the sins of the world was proclaimed. The church gathered in those who had ears to hear wherever they were found. It declared, moreover, that no earthly power had the right to interfere with the gathering in.

Here again, as with the exercise of congregational discipline the Free Churches have always found themselves in more or less direct conflict with the territorial and parochial system. The words of John Wesley in 1739, long before his societies left the Church of England, reveal just as surely the direction of his thought as do his teachings on baptism and the Lord's Supper:[10]

> You ask, How is it that I assemble Christians who are none of my charge, to sing psalm, and hear the Scriptures expounded? and you think it hard to justify doing this in other men's parishes, upon catholic principles. Permit me to speak plainly. If, by catholic principles you mean any other than scriptural, they weigh nothing with me; I allow no other rule, whether of faith or practice, than the holy Scriptures: but, on scriptural principles, I do not think it hard to justify whatever I do. God in Scripture commands me, according to my power, to instruct the ignorant, reform the wicked, confirm the virtuous. Man forbids me to do this in another s parish; that is, in effect, to do it at all; seeing I have now no parish of my own, nor probably ever shall. Whom then shall I hear, God or man? If it be just to obey man rather than God, judge me. A dispensation is committed to me; and woe is me if I preach not the Gospel.[11]

Just as surely as the Free Church is in tension with any religious establishment is it in tension with any form of culture religion. The typical culture religion of twentieth-century America pictures the individual Christian as a barefooted Spirit, and in practice accepts the control of outside cultural pressures and patterns in its thinking and acting.

When the churches settle down and attempt to avoid giving offense they are justly subject to criticism; thus, as was said of an earlier period, the Spirit of the World:

> by inoculating society at large with a very dilute and attenuated serum of Christianity, secured for it a measure of immunity from violent and inconvenient attacks.[12]

This charge is far more serious than the grievances of those spiritualizers who cannot bear the "offense of the Gospel."

Danger: A Facile Verbalism

Something has been said of the ideological situation in the public schools and in some seminaries. Nowhere is our problem more evident than in the pulpits. The purpose of preaching is to communicate; there must be something to be communicated if preaching is meaningful. Moreover, the sincerity of the spoken word is determined by the setting in which the pulpit is placed — i.e., in the situation of the congregation. An example of the popular pulpit will expose one danger. Some months ago an anniversary dinner was held in New York City to celebrate the long ministry of one of America's widely recognized preachers. At the commemoration a retired older colleague paid him tribute and explained his phenomenal popularity: One of the best-known preaching voices in America, his peculiar genius it has been to gather up the longings, the wishes, the unexpressed hopes, of large masses of people and give them back in literary form. No more damning thing could be said of one who at his ordination promised to maintain the form of sound doctrine, whose privileged calling it has been to preach Jesus Christ and Him crucified. The true preacher does not produce peace of mind for those who "sleep on beds of ivory"; he is much more apt to be denounced — at least once in a while — as a troubler in Israel. When John Wesley, one of the best-known men of his century, found himself late in his life accepted in churches formerly closed to him, he did not take it lying down. In his *Journal* entry for January 26, 1777, he wrote:

> I preached again at All Hallows Church, morning and afternoon. I found great liberty of spirit; and the congregation seemed to be much affected. How is this? Do

> I yet please men? Is the offence of the cross ceased? It seems, after being scandalous near fifty years, I am at length growing into an honorable man![13]

When a disgruntled parishioner complained to John Henry Newman (1801-90), whose eventual flight to Rome was in some measure in reaction against an acculturated English establishment, that his preaching was interfering with the man's business, said Newman: "Sir, it is the business of the Church to interfere with people."

The single quality most often lacking in contemporary American preaching is *moral earnestness:* that is to say, the conviction that the matters dealt with are desperately important and that a considered and guided decision by the hearers is essential unto salvation.[14] Preaching which is not "preaching for a verdict" is essentially frivolous, however blessed with other qualities of charm, wit, literary form and entertainment value. Preaching must have a "binding" intent, or it is better defined as lecturing.

Of course, customarily there is ample, indeed generous, attention to public and private problems; but as long as the discourse is "objective" (i.e., hands-in-pocket), it is not preaching.

> Concerning man in general, O Lord, thou knowest best;
> But concerning thy people, I will speak.

A distinguished ecumenical leader has described our habitual vantage point: "They speak to the *world,* as though *it* were the church."[15] But the pastor, in the privileged role of shepherd, is called to speak to the condition of the People of God. Talking over their heads to a larger circle of interested citizenry is popular, and frequently is appreciated by the attendants at worship precisely because it lays no concern directly on their corporate conscience. But in the end it is sheer irresponsibility in a man whom God will hold accountable for each of those given him in charge. "Feed my sheep!"

Our seminaries and churches have exaggerated the importance of a good voice and graceful gestures, and have emasculated the ministry of its essential character. The widespread theological illiteracy and ethical flaccidity so deplored in the churches is not primarily the fault of the laity: it goes back to a generation which has stressed promotional methods and verbal facility at the cost of intellectual and spiritual discipline. The shepherd's rod has a crook on it, and with that crook the true shepherd rescues those of his flock who have wandered down over the edge of the abyss. The sheep who is pulled bleating from the attractive descent is not always grateful, but the man who has been chosen to "bear all things" must include ingratitude and occasional resentment with his cross. He is not excused in taking up the role of entertainer by a general indifference to serious questions, or a popular resentment toward those who deal with them.

The emphasis upon charm and verbal facility has given us many natural-born leaders, blessed with magnetic personalities. A common result is the emergence of prophetic cults with a new revelation different from that given in Jesus Christ. This is evident not just in the "lunatic fringe" of tabernacle and tent sects, but in some of our major pulpits and university posts. The true preacher-pastor is preparing the way of the Lord, not gathering personal disciples; his is the spirit of John, who passed his followers on to Jesus — "behold the Lamb of God that taketh away the sins of the world" (John 1:36). He is content to be "a little pinch of salt" (Kierkegaard), or "as the filth and offscouring of the world to the glory of Christ" (Wesley). This is a very different thing from the "successful ministry" as popularly conceived and popularly acclaimed.

Danger: Loss of Discipline, Loss of Hope

The American churches, with occasional lapses, have long since won the major battles against persecution and outside interference; the battle against spiritualizing tendencies ranges today on a wider front than in previous generations. We might say that the major struggle of the pioneers of the Free Churches, against the persecutors and coercers of territorial Protestantism and Roman Catholicism in many areas has been won; but the minor struggle, against Sebastian Franck and Casper Schwenckfeld and their kind, has grown to unparalleled proportions. The partial triumph of a type of culture religion appropriate to well-meaning people in the mid-twentieth century can be seen clearly at two points: a) in the steady slackening off in internal discipline in recent years; and b) in the decline of Christian hope (eschatology).

The most pernicious influence tending to produce this condition is the dominance among Christian intellectuals, with a few encouraging exceptions, of an outdated theology: in many sections of the larger denominations, an antiquated nineteenth-century liberalism and, in few cases, an equally archaic fundamentalism. Among laymen and a few individual visionaries the primary influence is a transfer into the domain of the Church of a false idea of natural freedom of the individual. On the Continent, and to some degree in Great Britain, events of recent years have called forth a new thought and a new spirit; in America, with the exception of comparatively small circles, the larger denominations have yet to perceive again the cleft which exists between Christ and culture.

In some well-meaning groups a table of petty moralisms which limits smoking, drinking, dancing, and card playing is still considered definitive of a "good person" (i.e., a Christian). Much more common, however, is a two-dimensional identification of the genuine values of our society (freedom, free enterprise, communal responsibility, social justice, popular education, progressive thinking — the "democratic way of life," the "American way") with "being Christian." Promiscuity is widespread, not only between accepted social ideals and Christian ethics, but in the simplest organizational terms.

Take for a moment the matter of church discipline. In its series on "Great Churches of America," a series whose principle of selection in itself was revealing enough, *The Christian Century* reported on one large institution which takes in eight to ten persons a Sunday, most of whom have never been seen before. When the leaders are warned of the dangers inherent in such a mass approach, they say:

> Maybe. But what is a church? It certainly isn't a club of saints. We believe it is a fellowship of those who are seeking after righteousness, and we believe that when they knock at the doors of the Church, then is the time to swing them open and take them in. Our major responsibility starts once they cross that threshold. Our principle, in other words, isn't exclusion; it's inclusion, and then using every bit of resources we have here, both personal and material, to do the best job of Christian nurture of which we are capable.[16]

Whatever else we may say, these are the procedures and point of view of an established church. One is reminded of the protest of the Anabaptists against Hubmaier's practices at Nikolsburg (c. 1525), where fifty and sixty were taken in at a time without adequate preparation and without coming under the authority of the ban. The question arises whether, although legally "free," institutions with a promiscuous view of church membership are really Free Churches.

Or consider the matter of the Christian hope, which was so much the center of attention in connection with the Second Assembly of the World Council of Churches (Evanston, 1954). About the turn of the century two German professors of theology, at Berlin and Marburg, proclaimed their hope of things to come:

> It is not long since culture, rights and human dignity were the monopoly of some few thousand amongst all the inhabitants of Europe, while the great masses of people lived dreary lives under tyrannous oppression, possessing neither rights nor education, their whole existence being as one long misery. Today, on the contrary — at least in our own country, and among many other kindred nations — all citizens are equal in the eyes of the law; all enjoy the same legal protection; slavery and serfdom are things of the past; a fair amount of knowledge and education are within the reach of all; and labor is respected. Liberty, Equality and Fraternity are in many ways no mere empty words, but the real frame work of the building we are raising. All this has

> been accomplished in the life-time of a few generations, and it is absurd to question the fact of progress, amidst improvements so obvious and immense.
>
> Retrogression is no longer possible for us.[17]

This was, of course, before World War I, two depressions, and Adolf Hitler had brought about an "impossible" retrogression, taught some new lessons in the possibilities of slavery and serfdom, and brought upon the whole of Europe a sickness from which even the motherland of Liberty, Equality, and Fraternity has yet to recover. Yet, even in 1894, the relation of these phrases to the Biblical hope might properly have been the grounds for a closer scrutiny: social progress is not quite the same as Divine providence, and social amelioration along lines spotlighted by the Enlightenment is not, however desirable, identical with the Christian hope.

Elton Trueblood, in writing of the fall of France, made a telling point for Christian intellectuals:

> The vast importance of 1940 in our time lies in the fact that the weakness of an entire system in which we had great faith was then revealed to civilized mankind. The fall of France, though only one item in this historical situation, has been the most striking and the most shocking. France was a symbol of an entire kind of life that we had come to take for granted in the Western world. It represented the *urbanity,* the *individualism,* the *humaneness,* the *intelligence* that we had come to prize. Frenchmen were internationally minded, Frenchmen were relatively free from race-prejudice, Frenchmen were thrifty, Frenchmen believed in freedom of speech, freedom of thought, and freedom of worship. Here, it seemed, was the quintessence of Western civilization, which we had taken for centuries as our standard of comparison, and suddenly we realized that the new Rome was no more a match for the barbarian than the ancient Rome had been. In short it was demonstrated, in such a manner that all could see, that Western civilization lacked the security which we, in our innocence, had attributed to it.[18]

That all did not see and understand the demonstration is plain.

In a widely distributed book edited by Edward R. Murrow, in which one hundred leading Americans give their statements about the ultimate things, one encounters the following clues to the basic meaning of life:

> . . . a full, busy and for this reason happy life . . .
>
> . . . spirituality is the needed seasoning to America's materialism.
>
> I believe anyone can find a faith.
>
> Somehow the spirit of man will survive.
>
> . . . happiness is a truly basic objective.
>
> . . . to help create a social order in which persons are more important than things.
>
> I believe in people.
>
> . . . faith in human beings. . . ."
>
> . . . the validity of human rights. . . .
>
> rational intelligence. . . .
>
> character. . . .
>
> Freedom. . . .[19]

The mood of these short essays, with a few exceptions, can be termed at best that of courageous despair. Most of the men and women included in Murrow's book are churchgoers — but no one in their time has made clear the difference between the life of Marcus Aurelius and the life in Jesus Christ.

That the atmosphere is not much better in many professional circles of the churches was evident from various responses, some patently unfair and others simply bewildered, to the Preliminary Report for Evanston, which struck a frankly Biblical note:

> Our churches are sick. The sickness is shown in their

> being at home in the world and conformed to the world's standards. At the same time the churches are sick in that they are isolated from the world and are failing to speak to it.[20]

To the emphasis on hope, one clergyman in Iowa could only retreat to the nineteenth century, with the old saw that "The eschatological Christ has always been an escape mechanism for those followers of his who feel hopeless to do anything."[21] Without going into all corners of the Ecumene, the author feels competent to testify that in any comparison of effectiveness of social and political witness between the flat and uninteresting popular religion represented by the reverend brother and, say, the strongly eschatological orientation of the Kirchentag and Evangelical Academies of Germany, the latter will not suffer. One is reminded of the comment of H. Richard Niebuhr on the effects of the old-style liberalism in robbing the doctrine of the Kingdom of God of the eschatological element:

> A God without wrath brought man without sin into a kingdom without judgment through the ministrations of a Christ without a cross.[22]

After more letters and articles in the church press had revealed the extent to which American theology is still dominated by Schleiermacher, Ritschl, and Harnack, one younger pastor put a pointed question:

> But "realized," "futuristic," or both, where is the reputable modern New Testament critic who is non-eschatological in his interpretation of Jesus's teaching?[23]

The answer is that the leading scholars are again well ahead of the churches, and that most of the pastors of the larger denominations are now precisely where their teachers were a generation or two ago. If American laymen would demand intellectual precision of their leaders, instead of a slightly warmed-over serving of their own idealistic pap; if the religious bestsellers were less of corny miracles and amateur psychiatries; if the denominational leaders would give less attention to promotion and more to true teaching, less to verbal facility and more to pastoral concerns; then perhaps Almighty God would grant His Church a revival resting on something besides a panicky anti-Communism!

A Corrupted Liberalism

The author is perfectly aware of the debt which every believing man owes to textual criticism, to the comparative historical method, to disinterested scholarship in theology as well as the other sciences. He can only express his sympathy for those who are so situated as to have to argue about the inerrancy of the King James Version, the infallibility of Biblical zoology or geology, the mechanical operation of the assumption of Mary. But fundamentalism is not a threat to the faith; it is not even interesting. Totalitarianism is. And so is the "American religion," that bland confusion of Biblical and secular teachings which dominates many of the colleges and most of the seminaries of my own denomination. In this, it is only representative of majority Protestantism in the United States. Sociologically, it is a parallel to German Protestantism of the happy assumptions of 1871-1914; theologically, it is not markedly different from the *"positives Christentum"* of the *NSDAP* and *Deutsche Christen.* It is perhaps unfair to refer to this complex as the "liberal gnosis," since there *are* informed liberal Christians. But that the ignorance and incapacity of the Protestantism of the larger denominations, its lack of discipline, its lack of awareness of the meaning of the Nazi and Communist threats, its lack of eschatology, that this lack is enforced and justified by "liberal" dogmatism is everywhere evident.

No beating of the dead horse of fundamentalism, or assumption of a prior claim to social concern, can excuse this failure to come to grips with contemporary ideological and ethical issues. Liberalism in the German tradition was not unaware of social ills. Quite the contrary; there is a certain pathos in the way in which it attempted to alleviate them by passing resolutions. Ernst Troeltsch describes the functions of the Evangelical Congresses in the late nineteenth century in Germany, which show among other things that the problem of the spiritualizers can plague the establishments as well as the Free Churches:

> This comes out very plainly in the *Evangelischsoziale Kongress,* which is in itself so thoughtful and idealistic. Everytime it meets, the effort is made to formulate its Christian social ideas in a theological-ethical form, which will not be bound, like that of the sects, to the literal interpretation of the Bible, but which will express the "spirit of the Gospel," but which at the same time will not assert that the essence of religion is contained in the objective character of the Church as an institution, but which takes very seriously the ethical demands of the Gospel in the radical sense. In this, however, this movement has neither the sect community nor the Churches behind it; its supporters are solely individuals whose spirit is "Christian" in a free manner, but whose outlook is thoroughly in harmony with the modern elements in life. There is, however, no organized community in existence which embodies this "spirit;" in reality this spirit is first of all produced by a church or a sect, and it is only when it has severed its connection with both these forms of religious life that it becomes simply the "spirit of Christianity," which is a free principle, quite subjective in character, which, in the absence of any sociological basis of its own, finds it very difficult to do anything effective in social reform at all. At the same time this "spirit of Christianity" always experiences afresh the difficulties of coming to terms with the natural basis of human society. Its champions desire the spiritual interpretation of the Gospel, and the universality of a Christianity of the people, without the compromises of the Church and, without concealing the purely Divine element in the institutional character of the Church. Its champions desire the ethical radicalism of a Society which is built upon the ideal of the Gospel, without the narrowness and pettiness of the sect. It is, however, impossible to carry the "spirit of the Gospel" into practice without some opportunistic restriction to that which is practically possible, and without the resolve not to allow the best to be the enemy of the good.[24]

This quotation at length says everything which needs to be said not only about the Evangelical Social Congress in Germany, but about the variety of social action fellowships which meet annually in the United States to moralize and resolve on matters which in fact lie outside their areas of competence. The Church with integrity begins with an internal discipline before it carries its message to society at large. It does not, for instance, urge prohibition as government policy at the same time it refuses to make abstinence a matter of internal discipline.

The yearning toward vague interpersonal relations, indefinite in outline but surcharged emotionally, the sense of purposeful historical movement in a community but loosely limited, the religious mood but very vaguely related to a Biblical revelation from which all unique character has been removed — all were in full bloom in Schleiermacher and his romantic contemporaries, a century before National Socialism. The state becomes a living organism, a superpersonality whose duty it is to perfect its personality just as that is the duty of each individual. The essence of being and becoming is in this vital urge. The relationship of each individual within the state is one of function:

> However much remains undone, enough has been accomplished to make him feel lord of the earth, believing that nothing may be left unattempted in this, his own particular domain, that the concept of impossibility, ever narrowing, must finally vanish altogether. In respect to this purpose I feel that communion with mankind augments my own powers in every moment of my life. Each of us plies his own particular trade, completing the work of someone whom he never knew, or preparing the way for another who in turn will scarcely recognize how much he owes to him. Thus the work of humanity is promoted throughout the world; everyone feels the influence of others as part of his own life; by the ingenious mechanism of this community the slightest movement of each individual is conducted like an electric spark, through a long chain of a thousand living links, greatly amplifying its final effect; all are, as

> it were, members of a great organism, and whatever they may have done severally, is instantaneously consumated as its work.[25]

Wrote Schleiermacher in another instance:

> Every nationality is destined through its peculiar organization and its place in the world to represent a certain side of the divine image. . . . For it is God alone who directly assigns to each nationality its definite task on earth and inspires it with a definite spirit in order to glorify himself through each one in a peculiar manner.[26]

In view of recent history we may perhaps be forgiven the remark that in this inspired manner some nations are more "peculiar" than others!

It has become increasingly difficult in the early twentieth century to determine whether the "liberalism" in a certain type of liberal Christianity consisted in a vague style of social thinking or in doubt about what the Church confesses. With the rise of radical textual criticism in the late nineteenth century, with the abandonment of the Old Testament as "Jewish folklore and fable," with slighting reference in sophisticated circles to Paul as a "neurotic," the way was prepared for substitution of the Teutonic folk-myth as a new *Alttestament* and a "love ethic" of the German collective as a substitute for the fellowship of the redeemed. The national community, which had already taken on the mood of a religious fellowship, was thus providing a device for combining a simple synopticism with the more crude claims of folk-religion.[27] Jesus Christ, Judge of all men at the Last, was replaced by a Jesus who was supposed to have acted very much like an enlightened university man of our century. Of this, a man of faith could only say: "They have taken my Lord away, and I know not where they have laid him" (John 20:13).

"Culture Religion" in America

We are not yet so far along this road in America, but the theological factors are all there. And in the maintenance of certain standards of discipline, our larger churches are weaker than at any previous point in their history. Take this matter of racialism. One week in the summer of 1945 two contrasting items took the headlines. In one, the international officers of the United Automobile Workers (CIO) removed the west coast officers for refusing to admit Negroes to full membership in the region. In the other, a man who boasted that he was "a good Methodist" indulged on the floor of the United States Senate in violent abuse of the "kikes," "niggers," "dagoes," and so on. This moved the former president of the National Council of Methodist Youth to write:

> The recent "extended explanation" which Senators Bilbo and Eastland of Mississippi offered in opposition to FEPC prompts me to offer a suggestion. The Church ought to have sufficient ethical sensitiveness and power to reprimand or to remove from membership persons whose ideas and actions are totally contrary to Christian standards. In some congregations people who drink, commit adultery, or are divorced, suffer some penalties for their conduct. A more significant Christian ethic would be to somehow penalize men like Bilbo and Eastland and disavow the ideas which they expressed on the floor of the Senate on June 27, 28, and 29.[28]

We may be reasonably sure that Senator Bilbo was laid away as "our late lamented brother," and that no one has called into question in church councils the membership of the other public figure. Recently his blasphemous conduct again has indirectly become a public scandal in connection with resistance to the law of the land on equal justice to Negro citizens. There are certainly some who believe that Mr. Eastland has aided the Communists in his own way as effectively as Klaus Fuchs or Julius Rosenberg. So far as I know no bishop of his church has had the moral courage and faith to utter the more decisive word: that his conduct is a scandal before the face of our Lord.

Some time ago a meeting in a Methodist church at Mendenhall, Mississippi, adopted a resolution which plainly perverted Biblical teaching and tradition:

> We recognize the sovereign will of God in bringing to pass the various races of the world . . . that he lifts and casts down the races that he blesses and curses; that he sets bounds that they cannot pass; that he has forbidden as unwise the mingling of the races.[29]

It took the editor of the leading newspaper to condemn this heresy for what it was, a nasty American version of Hitlerism. But where was the bishop, the chief pastor, who was once set aside with the covenant "to hold fast the form of sound words, according to the established doctrines of the Gospel"?

There is another area in which, presumably, church members are more likely to agree: temperance. The Iowa Secretary of State, Mr. Rollo Bergeson, made a significant point in speaking some time ago to the Lutheran Brotherhood of Central Lutheran Church, Des Moines. As a member of First Lutheran Church in Sioux City he said:

> It is the oldest Lutheran Church in Sioux City. It is in the center of the one-time cheaper district. A good many of these . . . places were owned by members of our church. But did our church do anything either to stop the vice or to help its unfortunate human instruments? No. We blithely drove up to the church on Sunday and pretended that nothing like it existed.

Switching to the liquor traffic, he declared that

> no one can condone the action of men and women who ruin their health or their homes with over-indulgence of liquor.
>
> Yet, do you know how many of the vilest liquor dives in Des Moines are located in properties owned by churches or church members? The proportion would surprise you, gentlemen.[30]

It is not the intention of the present writing to urge prohibition on the government or teetotalism on the Church: it is to say that the handling of our ethic in regard to any ethical problem by means of annual resolutions at conference is, in the absence of any binding quality in those resolutions, something less than honest. More than that, it reveals the corrosive effect of a teaching on the role of the individual conscience which is a denial of the very meaning of Christian community. The Anabaptists of the sixteenth century were, in dealing with the spiritualizers and those individually illuminated at that time, engaged in a struggle over the very existence of the Church. The issues which confront us today in American Protestantism are no less severe. A good deal is written about the disintegrative effect of "sects," small religious enterprises more zealous than informed; but little is said about the pious individualism which denies, from the very pulpits of our churches, the existence of the binding fellowship in Christ.

The truth is that with our racially and culturally and economically divided denominations, with our secularized view of the meaning and direction of history, with our sentimentalism and moralism in the pulpits, we have as churches accepted the social status of establishments. Our major disciplines, in the larger denominations, are by and large those dictated by unbaptized influences from outside the fold. We prefer, therefore, the nice, dignified Jesus of the nineteenth century, who will not look too long upon our sins, but rather bless our half-formed and unimplemented idealisms. But when we seek to touch Him, he passes through the surrounding crowd to a place apart.

A View of Apostolicity

The pioneers of the Free Churches had very strong opinions about religious institutions which had settled back into the world, which had accepted the dictates of outside influences. The Church which had achieved worldly status by political and social acculturation was a "fallen" Church. The idea of the Fall of the Church has been a recurring theme in all "Left Wing" Protestant groups; the fact itself also may conceivably be a recurring phenomenon.

In his book on *The Church and the World in Idea and in History,* Walter Hobhouse expressed the familiar theme:

> Long ago I came to believe that the great change in the relations between the Church and the World which began with the conversion of Constantine is not only a decisive turning-point in Church history, but is also the key to many of the practical difficulties of the present day, and that the Church of the future is destined more and more to return to a condition of things somewhat like that which prevailed in the Ante-Nicene Church; that is to say, that instead of pretending to be co-extensive with the world, it will confess itself the Church of a minority, will accept a position involving a more conscious antagonism with the World, and will, in return, regain in some measure its former coherence.[31]

E. Stanley Jones reported, after the war, on a reforming bishop whom he had met in Latin America, a man expelled from the Roman Catholic Church, whose first purpose was declared to be "to go back to original Christianity, back beyond 270 A.D., before the councils arose, back to Christ."[32] The idea is older than Menno Simons (c. 1496-1581), although his emphasis on the "apostolic Christian Church," on "Jesus' Baptismal Command," on the "Teachings of the Apostles," on the "Baptismal Practice in Apostolic Times," was one of the most vivid presentations of it.

The idea of the Restitution of the True Church — that is, to redeem the "fallen" Church by restoring the order and life of the New Testament community — is another concept of "apostolicity," different from that which was common in the Roman Catholic and Protestant establishments. Richard Hooker (c. 1553-1600) rejected the newer doctrine of "apostolicity" out of hand:

> Concerning Rites and Ceremonies there may be fault, either in the kind or in the number and multitude of them. The first thing blamed about the kind of ours is, that in many things we have departed from the ancient simplicity of Christ and his Apostles; we have embraced more outward stateliness, we have those Orders in the exercise of Religion, which they who best pleased God, and served Him most devoutly, never had.

> Well assured I am they are far enough from acknowledging, that the Church ought to keep any thing as Apostolical, which is not found in the Apostles' writings, in what other records soever it be found. And therefore, whereas St. Augustine affirmeth, that those things which the whole church of Christ doth hold, may well be thought to be Apostolical, although they be not found written; this his judgment they utterly condemn.
>
> But to let pass St. Augustine, they who condemn him herein must needs confess it a very uncertain thing, what the Orders of the Church were in the Apostles' times, seeing the Scriptures do not mention them all, and other records thereof besides they utterly reject. So that in tying the Church to the Orders of the Apostles' times, they tie it to a marvellous uncertain rule.[33]

Quite obviously the concept of Apostolic Succession and the Anabaptist view of being faithful to the Apostles' model are two widely differing teachings. For the one, the touchstone of evidence is that body of tradition, in good part never committed to writing, to which appeal was recently made by the Bishop of Rome in proclaiming the dogma of the Assumption of Mary. For the other, there is a radical dependence upon the New Testament instructions — which are taken as earnestly in the matter of church order as in theology. Such a radical determination to reverse the direction of history and tradition would appear to lead into difficulties in relation to the continuity of Christian history. The problem thus posed, and the practical need to achieve a better understanding of the meaning of the term "apostolic" among the various wings of the ecumenical movement, will take some time to settle.

In the various groups of the Restitution there have been attempts from time to time to establish a new Apostolic Succession, in the more traditional sense of the term. A succession of Believers' Baptism from the time of the Early Church is one such line; if the break in history were believed to be irrevocable, a John Smyth (?-1612) [34] might try to re-establish it by self-baptism. The Nineteen Articles of the Collegiants, on the other hand, could declare the apostolic tradition extinct and set up a frankly human instrumentality of fellowship for which no special authority could be claimed. As John Smyth finally turned to the Dutch Mennonites in his quest for a valid succession, Thomas Helwys — Congregational pioneer — wrote to the Waterlanders:

> And the whole cause in question being Succession, (for so it is indeed and in truth) consider wee beseech you, how it is Anti-Christs cheife hold, and that it is Iewish and Ceremoniall, an ordinance of the old testament but not of ye new./Furthermore let it be well considered, that the succession which is stand upon, neither the time, Person, not place, can be proued to anie mans conscience, and so herein wee should ground our faith, wee canot tell vpon whome, nor when, nor where. . . . Wee beseech you consider how can wee of faith forsake ye euident leight of Gods truth to walke in such darkness.[35]

Smyth and his little group were then "churched" by the majority for having fallen away from pure congregationalism and the discipline which they had together instituted.

The essential matter would seem to be whether *some particular form* or *the fact of living in covenant* was to be taken as normative. The Hutterites and other wings of the Anabaptist movement, however, believed that the testimony of God had never been totally lost: during the period of the "fallen" Church the faithful little groups wandered like Israel in the wilderness. The pioneer Free Churchmen believed themselves to be heirs, therefore, of a valid tradition. They never would have tolerated the view that the Church is initiated by individuals, either saved or seeking salvation, and is therefore one among many human instrumentalities.[36] The Church was conceived of as the People of God. Certain rites and forms were important, according to their status in the Scriptures. But it is a mistake to profess that the essence of the Free Church tradition rests in some precise formula or institution. Immersion, for instance, dates from around 1640. The central teaching is, rather, that the Church is a divine community of disciplined fellowship; that it has continued throughout history and will remain until the final things; that within this covenant-people the Holy Spirit rules and establishes such order as He has declared, and continues to declare, appropriate to His flock.

Churches which have accepted some outside governance, whether political or cultural or by the spirit of the times, are not Free Churches in the proper sense of the term. Where, as very largely in America, the churches enjoy freedom from political control, they are not thereby justified in settling back into the accepted social standards. The final validation of their faithfulness is not in political freedom, but in Christian obedience, both in testimony and in behavior.

V. The Free Church vs. Totalitarianism

Protestantism not Individualism

Protestantism is frequently interpreted as an assertion of the principle of individualism, both in politics and religion. This has reflected on the part of some church historians the desire to attribute to their Evangelical tradition certain views of individual freedom esteemed by the modern mind, ideas which are in fact properly related to the Enlightenment and the French Revolution but very strange to the Reformers or the Free Churches. Among spiritualizers, from the sixteenth century to the present day, a type of atomism results which is compatible with philosophical anarchy and incompatible with church discipline. But these illuminated spirits have been, fortunately, in the minority in both Reformation and Restitution. As for the classical view, Peter Taylor Forsyth has written of Martin Luther and the Reformation:

> Religious Liberty . . . did not mean for him or his a liberty among men to choose your own religion; nor did liberty of conscience mean liberty to follow conscience in spite of society. It meant something higher and deeper — freedom before God by God's own grace in Christ. It certainly did not mean freedom to be free from God. The Reformation freedom therefore was not the republication of man's natural freedom revised, but the revelation of a new freedom only in the Gospel — a freedom by redemption, not creation.
>
> The Reformation did not propose as an end religious liberty in the political sense. It was not a battle for liberty but for Truth. It did not, and does not, care for liberty except as a product of the truth and for its sake. Truth is the Church's aim, liberty only a means thereto.[1]

It is a fundamental error to believe that Protestantism implies that "each may go to hell in his own way," or that the Protestant churches have been incapable of community in an organized sense.

The misunderstanding arises from the extent to which freedom in the political sense has been absorbed into the body of the Protestant churches, and also from the degree to which they have accepted outside political and social dictates in the life of the Church. In the measure, however, that the churches obtain a standard of true Christian obedience not only are they armed for carrying their mission in the world but by the nature of the case they are an offense to those quasi-religious political creeds which have their own mission and message of salvation. Thus the great leader of the Confessing Church, in his last sermon before a long imprisonment, cast individualism scornfully aside and defined the situation as a struggle between two kingdoms:

> Now we are fighting for the cross, for faith or unbelief, for the sovereignty of the crucified Christ or the sovereignty of the prince of this world. And we must not dream of peace, indeed we must not even hope for a truce, but we must clearly realize that we are being called upon to make a last bid for victory by the message of the Cross, which saves us from the power of the world and its prince and gives us the peace of God, so that we may not perish in this final battle, with its more than human temptations.
>
> Possibly the world can bear individual Christians, possibly it can tolerate the principle that each individual must be saved in his own way; but, as long as it wants to be itself, it cannot seriously want the Church of the Cross, but must fight against it in one way or another; and the more determinedly the world approves of itself, the more sharply must it resist a message which is based upon the belief that this world must pass away, nay more, that the judgment of God has already been pronounced upon it.[2]

The twenty-fourth article of the Nazi platform was, in

fact, a net for the feet of the unwary and a frank appeal to the individualists, the emancipated, the spiritualizers:

> We demand the freedom of all religious confessions in the state, in so far as they do not imperil its stability or offend against the ethical and moral senses of the German race. The Party, as such, adopts the standpoint of a positive Christianity, without binding itself confessionally to a particular creed.[3]

In their attack on the Church, the Nazis cleverly combined persecution from without and encouragement of internal disintegration. The real "church" had become, in fact, the nation; this national pseudo-religious community had a savior, a gospel, a scheme of salvation, and a millennium. The effect of the spiritualizers had been to remove the fence, weaken the faith in a historical hope throughout the Church, and prepare the way for a political collectivity with both discipline and eschatology. This was a political faith which a loose amalgam of pious individuals was powerless to resist. As Adolphe Keller wrote in *Church and State on the European Continent:*

> Let us remember here for a moment the individualism of the last century, which wrought such ravages even within the Christian Church. Coleridge said that he belonged to that holy and infallible Church of which he was the only member. In the new collectivity, on the contrary, the individual finds what the Christian Community was not giving him: a Church.[4]

Or, in the words of his younger colleague in the ecumenical movement, W. A. Visser 't Hooft:

> The main task of the Christian Community, and the greatest service which it can render to the world, is . . . to be the Christian Community. For the real tragedy of our time is that we have on the one hand an incoherent mass of individual Christians and on the other hand powerful impulses toward new forms of community, but no Christian Community. Christians today do not form a true Community, and the Communities which shape the new world are not Christian.[5]

There is a certain sense in which the Protestant principle implies a continuing reformation, an ever-new assertion of protest and the demand for reform. It is apparently because of this fact that Karl Barth has criticized so strongly the Hungarian Protestant leaders: "Do you see nothing odd in the fact that we in the west, your friends, swim against our current, but you so resolutely swim with yours — for about six years now?"[6]

Such an approach may be destructive of idols, established social patterns among them. On the constructive side, however, and plainly to be discerned in the history of the Free Churches since the Anabaptists of the sixteenth century, is the emphasis upon the Covenant, the community, the fellowship of believers, the Temple of the Holy Spirit. The issue between Protestantism and Roman Catholicism is not, therefore, individualism vs. discipline: *the issue is how that discipline is to be attained.* In those institutions with monarchical or bureaucratic structure, the discipline is determined by professionals and levied upon the members. In the Free Churches the laity comes into its own, and discipline is "talked up" among the members and made binding at the point where a consensus is obtained.

Totalitarian vs. Democratic Discipline

When discipline, democratically arrived at, is abandoned, our churches are in peril of their lives. The disintegration may come from within, as with the rise of spiritualizing personalities and movements; it may come from without, through "standing still" or succumbing to persecution. It has been the peculiar nature of the recent challenges to the Christian faith, both Nazism and Communism, to combine both the spiritualizing and persecuting tactics. The spiritualizer, often in open co-operation with the totalitarian government, seeks to dissolve the Church from within; the persecutors, often claiming to represent a "nonsectarian" type of Christianity, are not above establishing a "Counter-church" if it will serve their purpose.

The major tragedy of the present century of Christian

history is not that the churches are persecuted, for persecution is a recurring phenomenon. The tragedy is that the faith is opposed and persecuted by collectivities which have derived their strength from treason within the Church as well as from the skillful pirating and secularizing of powerful ideas and disciplines which are in fact indigenous to the Christian Community: group confession, the ban, sharing of the common life, eschatology, the doctrine of election ("the remnant"). These political collectivities were born and they also live from the apostasy of the Church. Rufus Jones once said that our churches are like Robinson Crusoe's goat pasture: the enclosure is so large that the goats within are nearly as wild as the goats without. In no other age of Christian history has the Church paid a larger penalty for promiscuity of mind and practice.

In one other respect current patterns of persecution are different in kind from those of former times: they are commonly backed by popular movements, and reflect the mood of mobs rather than the calculated policy of sober magistrates. Except for the Roman circuses there is scarcely a spectacle in history so pitiful as the denunciations and martyrdoms suffered by many North Korean and Chinese Christians with the triumph of the "People's Democracies." As long ago as 1914 Graham Wallas[7] warned that thought in modern times was becoming general rather than individual, that tired industrial populations were peculiarly susceptible to suggestion, that through subconscious conditionings persons were prepared for action in the mass. He did not know air travel and radio and television as we know them, as they have vastly increased the degree and breadth of control. But the real threat to political liberty and Christian Community today is not technological, any more than the true hope of man is a mythological science. The threat is from the increased potential of that sin which is in the heart of a man, the curing and control of which have been major tasks of the healing mission of the Church since the Christian beginnings.

The Persistence of Sin

The failure to take seriously the radical nature of sin and its consequences is one of the marks of culture religion, or of religious institutions which are prone to excessive optimism in regard to the regenerative value of unbaptized social forces. A grand concept has thus been eclipsed.

> In so far as this limited point of view prevails in the churches what have we? This: That sin has again shrunken down to little definite particulars, and this time to a mere handful of them. Why, in this way of guiding souls, the study of sin is not even a science of sorts, as it was in the Middle Ages; nor is its practice any longer an alluring act. Rather, sin has dwindled away to a short, unimaginative inventory of taboos, some of which are based on uncertain moral grounds to start with. So sin has come to this! We could say with a new meaning. "How are the mighty fallen!"[8]

But it is not alone among the laity that a superficial moralism has replaced the depth and wonder of faith. A typical statement of error, showing again the evil influence of an individualistic frame of reference, was perpetrated by one of the best-known American theologians in 1948:

> Now to our main question: How can an individual participate in a sinful society, without partaking of its sin, and in so doing, becoming generally as impotent as that sinful society? First, social participation is in grace, but never in sin. *There is no social sin and no social guilt.* There are social consequences of sin, even as there are social consequences of redemptive activity, but sin is ever an individual category. Before God, each must stand alone as a sinner. Sin is what separates. Grace is what binds together. In history man shares responsibility and consequences, but morally he is not held responsible for more than his opportunity of effective decision.[9]

As the churchmen who signed the Stuttgart Declaration of Guilt (Germany, 1945) were better aware, sin is a sticky and corrosive thing. The Anabaptist pioneers of the Free Church were voluntarists organizationally, but not theologically; they were too well aware of the pervasiveness of the Original Sin to suppose that either sin or salvation is an individual equation, escaping the God of nations and generations. And where Free Churchmen are true to their calling there is a deeper dimension to their thought than the lot of the individual. As John Horsch summed it up in speaking of certain groups in direct descent from the pioneer Free Churches:

> The Hutterites of our day believe that modern progress has changed neither the individual human heart nor the character of the world. For evidence they point to such facts as this, that the latest developments of science are to be utilized for unprecedented destruction of human life in war. The modern idea of Christ as the saviour of the world, in the sense that he is the leader in movements for world regeneration through reform, falls short by far of representing his true Saviourhood. He is the Redeemer of those only who have been personally saved, and in consequence own and follow him as their Lord. The world is to be overcome — not assimilated.[10]

Sin and the Role of Government

As Lord Bryce pointed out, the American Constitution — in contrast with the optimism of the statements of the French Revolution — was written by men who believed in the reality of Original Sin.[11] Discussion of the nature of sin in the human experience is not an abnormal deviation from an otherwise intellectual discussion of the nature of just and unjust governments. It is of the essence for a correct understanding of the problem. The political consequences of true or false faith are direct. Whether government is a necessary instrument to restrain evil and protect the good, or a living personality whose dynamic drive for self-expression invades every corner of existence, is a basic watershed of decision. The beautiful ideal State of Plato, and the organismic State of the romantic philosophers and totalitarians, are impossible concepts for the Christian. Speaking of this conflict of basic views, Ernst Cassirer wrote:

> The State could be justified to a certain extent, but it could never be rendered beautiful. It could not be conceived as pure and immaculate; for it always bore the mark of its origin. The stigma of the original sin was indelibly branded on it. That makes the sharp difference between classical Greek and early Christian thought.[12]

It also makes the difference between the pedestrian and restrained view of government which is found in English common law and in the thinking of the founders of the American Republic, and the various types of Utopianism/-totalitarianism which are today widespread.

To the Socialist Sir Stafford Cripps the duty of the "impartial" (Sebastian Franck's *"unpartheyisch"*) government in the time of the people's triumph is vigorously positive:

> The state is, in fact, accepted as the nearest that we can get to an impartial judge in any matter, though the degree of impartiality will, naturally, depend upon the nature of the controlling power in the State. If that controlling power represents particular interests, then the decisions of the State will tend to favour those interests against others; if, however, we have a true democracy in the State, then there is less liability for the State, to favour any particular section or class of the community.[13]

If the "State" (an abominable fiction!) , then, fails to act with true objectivity and fairness, this must be attributed to sinister pressure from various interested groups of classes in the population which seek to subvert the general interest to serve their own. The trouble with this hypothesis, which governs so much "enlightened" thinking today, is that it fails to take into account the most important force in the equation: the self-interest which also governs the men who make up the government bureaucracy itself. The triumph of the bureaucracy is to be seen in its most final form in Russia today: "What is demanded is approbation of everything done by the government." Of the workers, of whose destiny — with the triumph of the commissars at the expense of the Soviets — the bureaucrats became custodians:

> It is of course true that they are no longer exploited by shareholding capitalists, but nevertheless they are exploited, and in so devious, subtle and twisted a manner that they do not know any more whom to blame.[14]

Bishop Otto Dibelius, reviewing the Nazi tactic and pointing to present totalitarian trends and forces in middle Europe, summarized the matter brilliantly in his *Grenzen des Staates:*

> The over-reaching of state power means a secularizing of the life of the people. In relief and welfare, for instance, the question of material aid becomes dominant. In the school, the teacher's authority is undermined by denunciation from below. Labor is accented simply to increase production. *And in every area it now becomes the duty of the Church not simply to oppose power-conscious corruption with the truth, but to give examples of alternative forms of order.* In no place is this duty more pressing than in the education of children.[15]

Government is itself affected by the rule of sin, and not in petty defects or deficiencies but in ways all-pervading and often almost unrecognized. Those who think of government in restrained terms, who endeavor to fence its necessary function with checks and balances, are not laboring under an old-fashioned view of the state; they are informed by an old-fashioned — and still true — view of man's characteristic problems and possibilities. In reviewing the contribution of Edmund Burke to secure our liberties, against the political enthusiasts of his day, Crane Brinton has felt able to say that he

> . . . confronted in the French Revolution the kind of challenge we have confronted and still confront in the totalitarian revolutions of our day. He met that challenge by an appeal to the fundamental standards of our western civilization, an appeal which has itself helped clarify and formulate those standards. The debate between Burke and Paine, whose famous "Rights

> of Man" was a pamphlet in reply to Burke's "Reflections on the French Revolution," has been decided in favor of Burke as clearly as the debate over the relation between the motions of sun and earth has been decided in favor of Copernicus. . . . Anyone brought up in the Christian tradition should from the start be proof against the great error Burke spent his life combating, namely that human beings are born naturally good and naturally reasonable.[16]

Whether the larger denominations in America are as thoroughly purged of social positivism as are our best philosophers and ablest literary figures seem doubtful. It is one of the engaging ironies of the present situation that articles which deal at a profound theological level with our contemporary problems are as apt to appear in *The Saturday Review* as in *The Christian Century.*

Consensus vs. "Political Gnosticism"

In a society which avoids millennial overtones in its political decisions, the essential part of the enterprise occurs in independent centers of opinion where discussions point toward the reaching of a consensus. There is a fundamental difference between "talking up" and mere talk; the one reveals moral earnestness and the other leads to "political gnosticism." A recent report of the Committee on Christian Responsibility for European Cooperation (Brussels, October 2-3, 1954) highlights the problems of the churches:

> The Committee is deeply concerned that such a considerable segment of Christian opinion on recent political developments has frequently revealed an incapacity to discuss and decide in terms of concrete historical alternatives. This is particularly evident in some sections of the Church press. Many well-intentioned people are particularly prone to the temptation to consider historical events solely in terms of ideals. Responsible politics are, however, a modest and difficult enterprise involving mediation, compromise and the choice of the better of imperfect alternatives. Too often, the refusal to opt for the lesser evil contributes to the realization of the

> greater one. It is the duty of the Christian as a citizen to deal on the basis of the realizable. To disregard this often produces a politics of illusion which leads to the most disastrous consequences. This is to say that the angelic fallacy, sometimes called by political scientists "political gnosticism," shows up our basic spiritual sickness today.[17]

In the attempt to achieve an informed public policy in a democracy, when the process of attaining a consensus is followed all citizens affected participate — including those who simply sit on a balcony and say that the Kingdom of Heaven is better than any of the alternatives offered. That is to say, the process of creating an informed public opinion is one of the fruits of discussion pointing toward specific legislation; making law, in an "open society," is also creating the will to make the law operative. The failure of a certain type of mind to realize this fact is a perfect illustration of the lack of teleological or eschatological thinking, and results in a confusion of immediate possibilities and ultimate goals. It is, moreover, evidence of the failure of privileged and removed elements in the population to understand clearly the necessary and proper exercise of the magistrates' power. Teachers and preachers are especially prone to misunderstand the role of power in organized society, and to exaggerate the impact of the spoken word. Law has among its proper aims to make wrongdoing painful and costly, and to attain limited objectives of positive value.

That the positive objectives are *limited,* in this kind of a world, is in sharpest contrast with totalitarian pretensions. Three contrasting premises of democracy and totalitarianism have been stated by Eduard C. Lindemann:

> (1) Experience in the democratic way of life has, it seems to me, demonstrated that under democratic conditions there should never be an expectation of perfect realization of ideals. Democratic solutions, in other words, are always partial, never complete. Perfectionism and democracy are incompatible.
>
> (2) Democratic experience appears to have demon-

strated the fact that diversity is superior to uniformity. *E pluribus Unum* — through diversity towards unity — produces results which, when measured by humane standards, are better than those which follow upon rules of uniformity. *Gleichschaltung* is anti-thetical to the democratic ideal.

(3) Democratic experience seems to have provided assurance with respect to the doctrine that the means must, so far as possible, be consonant with the ends. The opposing doctrine which totalitarians espouse, that the ends justify the means, is unscientific before it becomes immoral.[18]

A citizen is not entitled to participate in the making of legislation by which he will later refuse to be bound; if he is a conscientious objector to all the alternatives offered, he must pay the price of his disobedience and console himself with the thought of the blessings of his final citizenship in a better world to come. But if he expects to be governed thereby, and to maintain active membership in the body politic, he should exercise his proper role in the attainment of a consensus. This process of government through consensus is in itself his most certain guarantee that he will not be the victimized subject of the type of regime which knows no limits to its ambitions or powers, which is anti-Christian in its very pretensions of sweeping competence.

Spiritual Resistance to Tyranny

The Christian theory and practice of spiritual resistance is one of the most debated issues today before the Church. In the Early Church, resistance to tyranny seems to have been restricted to the maintenance of strong internal discipline: prayer, preaching, sharing, fellowship, and excommunication all had their role in sustaining the Lord's People in their prevention of penetration by hostile forces, and in sustaining them in suffering and martyrdom. Martin Luther was profoundly opposed to use of the sword either to further the Gospel or resist the tyrant, an opposition modified only by his appreciation of the Schmalkald League. But his view of the princes' action was chiefly negative, that the proper lay magistrate might defend the churches against the power which wrongly sought to persecute and suppress them. With the intimate connection which came to exist between throne and altar in the Lutheran lands, Lutheranism has made almost no contribution to the Christian theory of resistance. Both Martin Niemoeller and Bishop Berggrav have been attacked bitterly within that confession for introducing uneasy thoughts about submission to the higher powers. John Calvin himself opposed any thought of popular revolt, although the magistrates might in executing their office resist a tyrant. Among Calvin's followers of the Huguenot fold, but more among the Scots Covenanters — where the idea of popular government had taken hold — the idea of open resistance even developed to the point of justifiable tyrannicide.[19] Ulrich Zwingli seems to have had no problem at all in pursuing religious objectives with armed means, being in this respect thoroughly medieval. Oliver Cromwell used the sword, and on occasion ruthlessly, but it bothered him; he was not, although it is so charged in some circles, a tyrant.

The Anabaptists of the sixteenth century, the first of the men of the Peace Churches (as well as Free Churchmen), developed their doctrine of spiritual resistance in the face of the most savage persecution. They could not have conceived of a representative government, hence could hardly have imagined a situation in which a tyrant should be overthrown in order to re-establish a just government. On the other hand, they were very far from the modern pacifist claim that pacifism "is the faith's core and condition."[20] Living in history, and dealing with very practical problems, they refused to escape persecution by "standing still"[21] and rebuked those who did. As with their repudiation of the "Maccabean" strain of Thomas Müntzer, their adoption of exile as a Christian witness (Matt. 10:23, 23:34) in preference to conventicle status preserved the integrity of their witness. In that period, almost all Christian subjects regarded the magistrate as a divine institution,[22] worthy of obedience in the interim until the Lord come again. The most that could be hoped for was a nonpersecuting government.

> Also we pray for all worldly government, that thou cause them to use the sword which thou hast given them to protect the good and punish the evil, and hold them back from steeping their hand in the blood of the innocent.[23]

The teaching is commonly called "nonresistance," to distinguish it from use of the sword in self-defense; the term "spiritual resistance," restricted to the struggles of the community against external and internal corruptions, is better yet.

> They must lay all iron and outward weapons away . . . and arm themselves with spiritual weapons.[24]

The formulae in memorials to the martyrs and on gravestones — "sealed his faith with his blood," "conducted himself in knightly form" — would seem to imply a more vigorous, though still nonviolent, witness to the truth than mere "nonresistance."

Spiritual Resistance vs. Modern Pacifism

In early Anabaptist/Mennonite thought the Christian kept his distance from government, usually for the best of reasons. His approach was vocational: the vocation of a Christian was that of a disciple, of a missioner of the Gospel.

> Further it was declared that it was not fitting for a Christian to be a member of government. Reason? The worldly government is according to the flesh, but the Christian according to the spirit. Their house and dwelling is fleshly in this world, the Christian's in heaven. . . . Their strife and weapons of war are fleshly and against flesh alone; but the Christian weapons are spiritual, against the fortress of the devil. The worldly are equipped with armor only against flesh but the Christians are equipped with the armor of God — truth, righteousness, peace, faith, salvation and the Word of God.[25]

The American Friends absorbed more of New World optimism, and participated more fully in the functions of government; but this has been a provisional participation. In 1756 the Quaker members resigned from the Pennsylvania legislature rather than vote for measures which conflicted with their peace testimony. They also resigned so as not to have to vote against these measures, recognizing that the colony had no real alternative, and that a stout resistance to the Indian depredations constituted a kind of "secondary good" to be respected as such.[26] The Civilian Public Service program is correlative with the Peace Church position, which does not expect too much of government and certainly does not confuse the demands that are on the Church with those on the magistrate.

Modern pacifism, mixed as it is with an optimism concerning history which is essentially Utopian rather than Biblical, is another story. There is in modern pacifism a constant note of irritation and pained surprise that the world turns out to be the kind of a place which the Bible says it is. The theological orientation, when present at all, is incoherent and confused. Thus, in a volume published some ten years ago by the Fellowship of Reconciliation, the author — after a fine exposition of the religious grounds for walking the way of Suffering Love — concludes:

> We who call ourselves pacifists and try to be Christians, have faith in the fundamental sanity and goodness of ordinary people in all countries.[27]

The shift from the Bible to Utopian thought is evident, but apparently this fits neatly into pacifist assumptions. The volume which Rufus Jones edited shortly before his death, *The Church, the Gospel, and War,*[28] contains similar evidence of confusion. When an appeal is made for clarification of the churches' stand on war and violence, it must come in proper form: i.e., as a testimony to the Church. Such questions cannot be settled, however, by appeal to a third party (as in self-righteous reference to those yet unconvinced as constantly wavering "in their allegiance between Spirit and the Works of the flesh" — Canon Raven), or by prudential philosophy ("no other way of dealing with sin has met with success" — Gliddon), or by attempting to prove that the incident on Golgotha's hill has after all turned out to be a success story. Contemporary pacifism has very frequently loaded its utterances with a measure of self-righteousness which is a far cry indeed from the humility and long-sufferingness of which the Bible speaks, and to which the fathers of the Peace Churches testified. No journal has been more guilty of this self-righteous utterance than *The Christian Century,* and a leading theologian has rightly protested:

> Some of us wonder how effective these polemics in the name of "love" are when they are based upon the pharisaical assumption that everyone who disagrees with you is a scoundrel and a coward who is merely capitulating to pressure. This is not an indictment of pacifists, many of whom are humble Christians. It is a protest against flagrant unfairness in argument by some pacifists whose "love ethic" has not generated ordinary decency in debate.[29]

The political consequences of self-deception are almost as dangerous as the spiritual consequences of self-righteousness. A few months before Chancellor Adenauer's overwhelming triumph in the Bundesrepublik elections (September 6, 1953), *The Christian Century* editorialized:

> A man who knows West Germany well predicted last week that in next year's elections not a single deputy will be chosen to the Bundestag who supports rearmament.[30]

The truth is, of course, that in its politics of the wish, in its moralistic style, in its lack of concern for internal discipline in the Church, this style of pacifism is an organic part of that spiritualizing thrust which has so weakened and exposed the churches to internal disintegration precisely at the time when they are confronted with totalitarian threats of a ferocity unparalleled in Christian history.

What, then, is the contribution of "integral" Christianity to the struggle against totalitarianism? Is it in some secret clue which unlocks a new power, and overcomes the adversary by a weapon against which there is no adequate defense? This might seem to be implied in Ethelbert Stauffer's interpretation of the Anabaptist theology of suffering:

> But the martyr's death of Stephen, in which the situation sharpened up by the experience of Christ appeared for the first time and as a lesson, not only showed that the witness must according to Christ's example take upon himself suffering and death, but also *how* he should do it. He cried . . . according to the manner and model of his Master on the Cross: "Lord, do not count this sin against them!" This is the new standpoint according to Christ's saving act, with which the redeemed overcome their fate, their opponent.[31]

For a moment it appears we are led back into the gnosis of modern pacifism. But what was being taught here was not a theory of power and government. Rather it was a testimony to the fact that death itself can be a bulwark of the mission to gather in the harvest to the Lord.

The Free Church Contribution: Five Areas

What can the "nonresistants" contribute to the battle of the Church against totalitarianism? The query is a most serious one, and it is one to which the churches with a long history of spiritual resistance should have some answers. Particularly is this true at a time when the real encounter is not political or military so much as ideological.

The *first* area would seem to be in the skills and methods which characterize a well-disciplined laity. (The laity first came into its own with the Free Churches.) For instance, a recent report from Communist-controlled East Germany points up the need for a laity with initiative and staying power:

> The attack from the Hitler State was launched against the ministers of the church. The ministers bore the brunt of the anti-Christian attack. In the church of the East Zone today the lay people have to carry the burden. The lay people find themselves at the frontline of de-

> cision, rejection or acceptance. The ministers are exempted from the necessity of belonging to the Party or other political organizations. In a sense they are being segregated. This looks like a tactical move on the part of the State. The State hopes to drive a wedge between the ministers and their parishioners. There are many ministers who say: "It is easier for us to preserve a relatively undisturbed conscience. We are not forced to join. But our parish members always feel the direct pressure of the political Gleichschaltung."[32]

The Free Churches from the beginning have held the viewpoint — in opposition to the clergy-centered establishments — that the life of the Church centers in the people and the congregation. During the period of struggle with Nazism, certain Christian resistance groups in the Netherlands, Norway, and Germany were forced into the position of free churches. They were ill-equipped to meet the change, as are the disestablished and pressured churches today in some Communist lands. (Under the Communists of Czechoslovakia the churches have been established legally and controlled to an unheard-of degree. The tactic swings between extremes.) The Christian churches which today live under "the sign of the fish" need help in developing an informed and capable laity. The methods of discussion and reaching decision, the decentralization into the local congregation, the sharing fellowship which makes persecution less onerous, the disciplines which maintain the integrity of the Church under the guidance of the Holy Spirit — all must be learned anew in whole or in part.

Second, the recognition of and resistance to distintegrative ideas and appeals is a skill in which the Free Churches were once well versed. The youth is a special target of the totalitarians. At the Denver meeting of the National Council of Churches (1952) Bishop Otto Dibelius pointed out the appeal:

> The Communists do not differ one bit from their predecessors, the National Socialists. The youth is the target group for their propaganda. Young people are put in

> responsible positions. It is not extraordinary that a 22-year-old becomes mayor of a town of 100,000 people. There are railway stations designated as railway stations of Free German Youth. There the station-master may be 18 years of age, and all who work with him are younger. Such things impress youth. Therefore, the whole ire of the Communists is poured on the youth work of the church.[33]

In 1950 Bishop Hahn of Saxony wrote of the condition of the younger children in the Communist-controlled schools:

> It is becoming continually more evident that education in the school has a wholly secular trend, which stands in open contradiction to the church's freedom to propagate the gospel, guaranteed under the Constitution. In several cases of conspicuous non-observance of this right, the Ministry of Education accepted the Church's protest. In most cases, however, protests cannot be made, because in the event of a dispute arising one would have to depend heavily on the testimony of school children. It is rather a matter of an alien spirit, which the children sense, without being able to do much about it. Baptized children are growing up in a world in which, despite the efforts of catechists and preachers, they are inwardly ground to pieces.[34]

Such a concentration upon the coming generation reveals the essentially millennialist nature of the Communist, like the Nazi, dispensation. In the Church, however, the covenant between fathers and sons is emphasized, and the family is the center of both faith and education. The drive to control the youth by the state stems from a false ideology, and in contrast accents the importance of the family and the role of the Church as the Covenant of families for the faithful.

3 *Third,* just as a democratic society is strengthened by the activity of a wide variety of independent centers of leadership, finance, and program, so a totalitarian system is hostile to it. The society in which the voice of the people takes the place of God, in which all dynamic purpose is centered in the state, has found churches and synagogues, trade unions and

business associations, co-operative societies and lawyer's guilds, dangerous to its existence. The elimination of voluntary associations was a definite strategy of the National Socialists and it is pursued just as vigorously by the Communists.[35] In the totalitarian society all is bureaucratized; the central government is like Moses' rod which swallowed up all the lesser serpents of the magicians. In a situation where the state aspires to be a church, the True Church must hold its lines with redoubled vigor. The necessity of a thoroughgoing structure of democratic discipline is underlined. The laity takes its proper place at the center of the Church. Of basic importance is the problem of a defined membership; i.e., whether members of government in a totalitarian system can be accepted at communion ("the lesser excommunication"), or as members in good standing at all ("the greater excommunication"). The territorial churches are at a heavy disadvantage in facing this issue, whereas the lessons of Free Church history are relevant and readily available.

Fourth, it must be recognized that in this confrontation we are dealing with a secularized religion. Whereas in our own society the political air has been freshened by the adaptation to political life of some theories and methods which came from the Free Churches and their ways, in Nazism and Communism there have been revived certain practices and doctrines neglected by the churches and now turned against their original source. Consider the doctrine of election, of the function of the remnant which carries history. The Christendom described in Thomas Mann's *Buddenbrooks* wanted to know nothing of a concept with such energetic implications. Establishments in Europe, and the churches in America to the extent that they have become socially established, have abandoned the teaching of election and the practical implications of it. Even certain sections of Judaism, and Jewish peoplehood is to a marked degree a testing point for culture religion both quiet and demonic, have dropped the teaching and settled into a homogenized pattern.[36] But in this, as in some other matters, "the children of this world are in their generation wiser than the children of light" (Luke 16:8). The thoroughly thought out distinction between "members" (who are disciplined and bear the brunt) and supporters (who come along when the going is good) is Hitler's most original contribution in *Mein Kampf*. And along with the distinction comes the lines between "organization" and "propaganda." The core, the striking power, of the movement was kept small and thoroughly trained. In facing Communism, one turns immediately to Lenin's intense program for the Vanguard: "Strict secrecy, strict selection of members, and the training of professional revolutionaries."[37]

The understanding that history is carried by a chosen people, a disciplined remnant, is — after all — Biblical. The function and effect of the creative Vanguard, which Engels and Lenin pitted against idealistic views of society and power, is here significant as the secularization of the record of the Messiah-people of the Hebrew-Christian world-view. History is moved not by "men of good will" nor by their ideas, but by those who are prepared to harness flesh and blood to make concretely evident the idea whose time has come. This teaching on the importance of discipline may not inspire masses of churchmen, but it is imperative for those who are not content to let the new secular religions sweep the field.

The teaching is important, and the methodological consequences are important. In the words of Paul Tillich, writing during World War II:

> Although the churches as large social institutions have adapted themselves to the great historical transformation — sometimes, as in the Middle Ages and the Reformation, even in a leading role — they have not completely surrendered to the given social structure. They still resist a complete subjection to the trend towards dehumanization and mechanization. But more important, they have preserved the message of an ultimate meaning of life which has not yet been exhausted and which, as Christians believe, never can be exhausted. However, this message can become effective for the coming spirit-

> ual reconstruction only if it is brought into the center of the present situation as an answer and not as another problem tied up with the general spiritual disintegration. This cannot be done by the churches officially; it is an adventurous task and the duty of a Christian vanguard of a voluntary and half-esoteric character. The authority of the churches, especially in their ecumenical unity, may be behind those who go this way. But the churches themselves are too much bound by their traditional forms on the one hand, and by their amalgamation with the present structure of society on the other hand. The support and protection of a spiritual language will be the main contribution of the churches to the spiritual reconstruction after the war.[38]

Europe's sickness, and America's partial ill health, has been but increased by the war; the peril, in one form diminished with the collapse of National Socialism, has grown in another. That a Christian-Marxist Institute can be today led by a professor of theology at the once great university of Leipzig, with the expressed purpose of harmonizing incompatibles, is not simply an academic riddle. It lays upon the conscience of the Church the need for a renewed discipline and sense of mission. Such discipline must be taken up by the congregations and councils where possible, and by creative minorities in situations where the static element triumphs for a time.

Finally, the maintenance of the bonds of fellowship across national lines and geographical distances has become a matter of both principle and strategy. Technologically, the world has become small and explosive. The prayers and fraternity between the churches are needed as never before to hold it together. The lessons of the Free Church way, on the mission field and under the totalitarians, have become doubly important. Many of the former persecuting churches are ready to enter into joint discussion, study, and prayer. This means that those of the Anabaptist/Mennonite tradition have, in a situation where the achievement of consensus is a basic approach to understanding between the churches, a special responsibility. To say the least, it justifies a different attitude and approach and distance from that maintained toward the persecutors — whether church establishment of an earlier age or political ideologies of today.

A leader in the ecumenical movement has summarized the common predicament of the churches in this generation, whether of the traditional pattern or free:

> The "Front" of the Reformation, which justifies its one-sidedness of accent, is no longer that on which we are fighting. We are confronted, not by a false doctrine of freedom, but a false determinism; not in the first place a false humanism, but a false naturalism; and — if I may coin this word — a false "cosmism." Therefore it is today especially necessary to advance against this enormous power of a paralyzing belief in fate with the witness that was the battle-cry of the elder Blumhardt — "Jesus is Conqueror!"

Further, he writes, the faith must be completed:

> The Church is the fellowship of those who not only believe in the forgiveness of sin, but also in the consequence of this faith experience — renewal through the Holy Spirit.
>
> It is not fanatical enthusiasm but lack of faith which is the chronic disease in the Church. The Church has not believed her Lord's saying that he would do even greater things through his disciples than he had done himself. Only too easily has the Church been content with believing that the time of miracles was once and for all past. But as long as real miracles happen, and wherever they happen in the Church, then it is obvious that men will speak about them.[39]

Although we may feel that the danger of a false freedom is greater than here indicated, there is no question that in the face of false "cosmisms" the various lines of the Christian tradition are being brought together today as never before. In the conferences and common action which marks this encounter, those true to the Free Church tradition have much to share. Free Churchmen should, to be specific, support the ecumenical movement, and with it the brethren who live under "the sign of the fish."

VI. The Free Church and Its Discipline

"Bindingness" in the Church

In the midst of the Church struggle with National Socialism, Karl Barth made a plea for that striving toward a consensus, that bindingness of address, that loyalty to the Community and its discipline, which alone can arm the faithful to stand firm and to witness steadfastly.

> The Church of which we have been speaking is the Evangelical Church in which no one has the right to hold back with his witness and confession until the contents of this are pronounced *de fide* by some higher Church-Court. But also for this reason no one has the right to complain when he must listen to such a witness and confession, even although at first this is not yet his own! And he has also no right to complain when he must hear and take notice that the other is *not* bringing forward what he has to say as a personal—where possible "only" political—expression of opinion; but that he is bringing it forward in proper form, i.e. in unity with the confession of Jesus Christ, as he sees this, and hence in all seriousness as true and *binding*. Can there and may there be in the Church speech which is not *binding*? Would it be a witness and confession, if I did not thereby make the "unreasonable demand" of the other that he agree with me? Would we do one another honour by dispensing with this "unreasonable demand" and limiting ourselves to pure expressions of our own personal opinions? What have we to say to one another if we do not dare to speak bindingly with each other? Is not the very fact that so wretchedly little binding address is heard in the Church accountable for a goodly share of her misery—is it not perhaps *the* misery?[1]

Seldom has the finger been put more accurately on the sickness of our churches, both European (legally established) and American (socially established).

One has only to live through our church conferences in the larger denominations to appreciate the point. Every year, for instance, the little group of pacifists will bring a set of resolutions to the floor of the several regional and national assemblies. A quarter of a century ago and before, these same resolutions provoked the most earnest debate. Ethical, and even theological, issues were fought out with passion, intelligence, and a certain measure of brotherliness. Today such resolutions go through with scarcely an opposing voice. Why? Has the denomination suddenly become pacifist? Hardly, for the resolutions do not in fact represent 10 percent of the membership. The reason these statements are allowed to go through is that everyone knows they don't make any difference anyway. If it makes the Commission on World Peace feel better, why not? "After all, it's only a personal opinion." If a delegate wants to enjoy the intellectual wrestling of a real debate, he must get into the discussions on appropriations and expenditures. For in this field every decision is a real one, affecting the life of the entire membership.

The newness of the American religious situation — for the first time in history the religious discipline of millions of people is exclusively a matter of internal decision, the attractiveness of American society in so many aspects — has brought about a situation in which every season sees a diminishing of the caliber of intellectual and ethical discipline wherein church memberships are willing to bind themselves. Yet freedom in doctrine and living has never been a part of the major tradition of the Free Churches; it cannot be too often or too strongly emphasized that the basic element was *not freedom,* but the *freedom to participate* in the discussions by which discipline was arrived at democratically. Nor is excessive "freedom" attractive to those who are dissatisfied with pious petty rules and a callow philosophy of material success. The very considerable number of able young people of Europe who became Nazi or Communist activists in the twenties and thirties, and the number of my generation who left the churches for the co-operatives and trade unions and pacifist and Socialist crusades, can be charged in large part to the failure of older church leaders to shepherd faithfully, to speak bindingly, and to proclaim hope in the God who keeps His promises.

In an appeal to the Church, one sensitive young laywoman wrote some fifteen years ago:

> As the crisis of our age nears its climax we sincerely desire that we may not be caught, like the baffled religious and non-religious liberals of most periods of severe social change, in a futile backwash of good intentions. Neither do we wish to withdraw from our spiritual mother, the Church, and identify ourselves with some purely materialistic revolutionary movement. By and large, we are lay men and women, rather ordinary folks, but in deep need of some sort of "Third Order" like the Third Order of St. Francis. We need guidance and leadership.[2]

There is as yet little evidence that any of the larger denominations has considered seriously the implications of such an appeal, and there have been many such appeals from youth and student conferences and organizations over two decades.

The Penalty of Promiscuity

A thousand years ago the Church faced another challenge, and many sections failed to face the intellectual and organizational issues squarely. In the Report of Commission IV of the World Missionary Conference at Edinburgh, 1910, there is a striking passage on the relation of Christianity to the spread of Islam:

> . . . it remains tragically true that had the Church of Syria been faithful to its Master the reproach of Islam had never lain upon Christendom. The thought has sombre consequences. It may be that in the Africa, the China, and the India to-day new religions are maturing which in like manner will be "anti-Christian," and

> stand in future centuries as a barrier in the way of winning the world.[3]

The criticism of the Church of Syria is not the primary concern here, but rather the warning. Upon reflection, and guided by the self-examination recent decades should have taught us, it strikes home that precisely that happened which had been warned against. But the demonic upthrusts did not come initially in Africa or India, or even China: they arose in the very heart of Christendom! In the shock of that realization we may well ask ourselves wherein was the apostasy of the west, in what was "Christendom" so remiss, that when the new religions matured they came at the center of the Christian world rather than at the periphery or among the lands of the younger churches which evidently had worried the Commission. This fact is the scandal of our time. This question is the sword which pierces the heart of all who love our spiritual mother, the Church.

What has happened, in the acculturation of Christianity in both Europe and America, is a growing promiscuity of membership standards and frivolity of preaching and practice. That the Free Churches, whose original complaint against the establishments was precisely that they practiced no true Christian discipline, should have succumbed to such a degree is a scandal twice compounded.

American Statistical Success

The situation in America is still different from that in the lands with establishments of declining influence and authority. When Mass Observation surveyed the matter of loyalty to the Church in the population of Britain during the war, the staff reported:

- 1/10 active in the churches
- 1/10 thinking the Church would play a larger role following the war
- 3/10 who would welcome such a development
- 5/10 indifferent or hostile in attitude.[4]

In the United States, however, neither statistical membership nor attendance at services is the basic problem. Hostility to the churches is almost absent. A scientific survey of attendance brought out the following facts at the end of the war:

Weekly attendance:

Roman Catholics	69%
Protestants	36%
Jews	9%

Monthly attendance:

Roman Catholics	81%
Protestants	62%
Jews	24%[5]

Furthermore, the growth of statistical membership in the American churches has been one of the most startling phenomena of American history since independence.

By the end of the establishments of the colonial period, church membership had fallen to some 5 percent of the population. In 1800 it had risen to 6.9 percent; in 1850, 15.5 percent; in 1900, 35.7 percent. The United States was not "Christian," even nominally, in the founding fathers' generation toward which some look back so romantically. It was not until the census of 1926 that a little over 50 percent claimed church membership.[6] According to a subsequent survey, the tremendous influx has continued: from 1926 to 1943-44, church membership increased by 32.8 percent, while local churches increased only 9.3 percent in number and the population grew 13.9 percent.[7] Christianity, in the formal sense, is hardly declining in the United States. On the contrary, we are at the high tide of a century and a half of revivals and mass movements comparable only to the way in which hundreds of thousands from the Germanic tribes accepted baptism in the eighth, ninth, and tenth centuries of the Christian era. And herein lies our problem.

When the pagan hordes flooded into the Church of the late Roman Empire they brought with them the blind superstitions and vile brutalities of their unregenerate life. It took centuries to distill out a high quality of Christian civilization. There still are sections of European Christendom where the pagan shrines have been blessed and preserved intact, to mention only one evidence of persistent heathenism. So it is in America today: the millions of new church members have carried over bodily into their congregations the race prejudice, the adulation of size and statistics, and the disrespect for tradition, duly constituted authority, and government, which mark American society at large. The basic task before the churches is precisely one of Christian discipline: to create within the congregations of new Christians that quality of consecrated thinking and obedience which is appropriate to a Biblical people.

The Price of Success

The degree of ethical and theological illiteracy in which American Christianity founders can be measured in many ways. For instance, many of the brightest and best individuals affect an indifference to loyalty to the Christian Community: "I don't care what he thinks, or whether he goes to church, so long as he behaves himself and 'lives right.'" What a "good person" is, and how he behaves, comes readily to be judged by sub-Christian standards, or even anti-Christian admiration of "success," enterprise, personal conquest, and perhaps "conspicuous consumption." The fullness of life in Christ — which is the duty of the Community bearing His name — is hardly to be realized by emancipated individuals who are parasitical upon a tradition they will not help to carry. Further, if ever a proposition were proved to the hilt it is this: that "ideas" (that is, incarnated ideas) are "weapons," and it matters profoundly what a person believes and what community shapes his views of life issues. We know that if man's thoughts are not conformed in Christ they will be shaped by some other association. In our modern world of instant communication the fatal power of false ideologies has been angrily demonstrated.

The initial advantage of the American pattern over against the European was summarized many years ago by the great church historian, Philip Schaff:

> In large cities on the Continent there are parishes of fifty thousand souls with a single pastor; while in the

> United States of America there is on an average one pastor to every thousand members.
>
> The free-church system secures the exercise of church discipline, which is almost impossible in state-churches, and provides a purer and more efficient ministry.[8]

It is therefore doubly dismaying to read the following statement about our educational methods of the children and youth (a statement not true for all churches since the appearance of the Christian Faith and Life Program of the Presbyterians):

> The average farmer has more accurate information about the number and characteristics of pigs and cows that he owns than the average church school has regarding its members.[9]

Equally incredible is a report from what claims to be the largest church in America, in which an "estimated constituency" of some 12,000 individuals is recorded.[10] This is spiritually on a par, to use a form of expression which occurs frequently in the Bible, with a man's remarking that he is the father of an estimated number of children. The sin of promiscuity is not only a personal matter.

An Example: Christian Discipline vs. Racialism

The first duty of the church is to be the Church ruled by the Holy Spirit in residence, under the Headship of Jesus Christ. When the Roman Catholic Church in St. Louis several years ago ended segregation in the parochial schools, and her hierarchy enforced obedience to the point of threatening excommunication against a group of resisting white parents, *The Christian Century* reported:

> The attitude of liberal Protestants generally holds that Archbishop Ritter accomplished a good thing by a means that all Protestants must despise.[11]

The remark reveals the typical contemporary confusion of Protestantism and individualism. A more representative statement in the Free Church tradition is this from the South Carolina *Federated Forces Bulletin:*

> Any Protestant Church is justified in expelling from membership anyone who unites with the Ku Klux Klan or subscribes to its doctrines of hate, prejudice and the use of force. "The cross was made to be borne, not to be burned."[12]

When a church accepts cultural or national disciplines in preference to the New Testament order and brotherhood it is guilty of treason to her Lord. And in all lands, with varying degrees and types of unbaptized thinking and conduct, a people which takes its calling seriously must have the high courage and stout faith to accept the yoke and harness of Christ. This has never been easy. It may be part of the prophetic mission, which is now (in the Christian era) the burden of the Church rather than the prerogative of individuals. To give an example: at Bloemfontein, South Africa, on the Day of the Covenant, 1952, an interracial service was held at the Anglican Cathedral. Dean Findley said the service, illegal in that unhappy land, was "to witness to a vital and uncompromising truth, that we are, whether African, Colored or European, all one in Christ." In his sermon he further commented that too many church members refused to take a firm and principled stand on racialism and instead "accept the voice of the people as the voice of God."[13] It is precisely the scandal of the dominant religion of the Union of South Africa that her people are unclear as to whether the true Day of the Covenant is a cultural and historical accident or a Divine event which occurs wherever men and women — of whatever tongue, race, nation, or geographical division — are gathered about the Hill of the Lord to hear His Law and obey His Will.

A principled stand may meet criticism from the spiritualizers within the "membership." For example, when the Church of England in Australia considered recently the reintroduction of rather elementary regulation to govern the use of the rites of the Church, a magazine of the Church in the homeland commented unfavorably. The recommendations so commented on were:

(1) that baptism be refused a child neither of whose

> parents is a regular worshipper; (2) that the rite of Holy Matrimony be refused where neither party is fulfilling the duty of worship; (3) that it is a farce, and not a charity, to read the burial office over one who has persistently separated himself from the fellowship of the Church, and to refer to him as "our dear brother here departed."[14]

But, whether in tension with social norms or in conflict with disintegrative factors within the fold, the basic fact still remains:

> Only a church that believes in and practices discipline maintains the sanctity of the body of Christ. A church in decay is a church without discipline.[15]

It is too much to expect that a church body which does not maintain the most elementary internal integrity will be capable of maintaining ethical and moral and intellectual standards superior to those of the surrounding society.

Community as an Educative Factor

The importance of the community experience, both in maintaining a firm position and in the process of learning, has been amply documented by contemporary social psychologists. In the learning process, an individual's changes of attitudes and opinions reflect primarily the situation in which he finds himself. In an essay, "Conduct, Knowledge, and the Acceptance of New Values," Kurt Lewin stated the matter quite conclusively:

> *Acceptance of the new set of values and beliefs cannot usually be brought about item by item.*
>
> *The individual accepts the new system of values and beliefs by accepting belongingness to a group.*
>
> *The chances for re-education seem to be increased whenever a strong we-feeling is created.*[16]

One of Lewin's friends and associates, now a professor at the University of Michigan, came to similar conclusions after a five-year study of an American college.[17] Some of his conclusions are particularly illuminating. He found that at the end of the period there was no measurable correlation between the courses taken, lectures heard, books read, and the changes of attitudes and opinions on certain significant public issues. On the other hand, there was an almost 75 percent correlation between the individual's attitudes and opinions and those of the friendship group to which he belonged. In short, the learner changed by the working of "the thoughts which wound from behind" (as Kierkegaard put it), by the indirect and frequently unconscious appropriation of attitudes and ideas of the group which he admired and aspired to be like. The only comfort for the lecturer, the professor who used formal classroom methods, was that he might be a member of the friendship group. In that case, he would of course have a wider influence because of his stronger personality and greater knowledge. In short, those who stress a purely individualistic approach to ideology and virtue, or are enamored with the value of discarnate ideas, are out of date pedagogically as well as dangerous theologically. The function of the Church as the School of Christ is confirmed.

The Japanese have two proverbs which are here appropriate:

> You don't fill a stand of narrow-necked bottles by dumping a bucket of water over them.
>
> It is no use to throw eye medicine out of a second-story window.

In the disciplines which accompanied the Anabaptist Restitution of the True Church,[18] the fathers of the Free Church movement showed their awareness of the downward tendency of man in his natural state and the necessity for exercising pastoral care at strategic points. The early Methodists also were of the same realistic school of thought. In an early edition of *The Discipline* of the American Methodists (1798) we read:

> Our society may be considered as a spiritual hospital, where souls come to be cured of their spiritual diseases.

> The members therefore who compose our class meetings vary exceedingly in the state of their minds and the degrees of their experience. On this account it was thought necessary by our venerable leader Mr. Wesley, to establish a society of evangelical believers within the society composed of the whole body of Methodists, to which he gave the name of *the band-society:* This institution he borrowed from the practice of the primitive churches, as indeed he did almost everything he established.

Discipline was established in this developing Free Church, therefore, not to enthrone a set of petty negatives,[19] but for the purpose of building spiritual health and strength. Beyond that, a democratically disciplined community was capable of spiritual warfare.

Community and Separation

The Free Church fathers were convinced that separation from the world and its pressures was essential in order to accomplish a rigorous internal discipline, and that the community of the elect was restoring the New Testament pattern in setting up a fence between the sheep pen and the world.

> Fourthly, we are agreed concerning separation. It shall be: from the evil and unrest that the Devil has planted in the world; plainly therefore we shall not have community with them and run with them in the mass of their abominations. . . . Now there is also evident the command of the Lord (II *Cor.* 6:17f) in which he instructed us to be separate from evil; then would our God be a friend, and we his sons and daughters. Further he warned us (*Acts* 18:4f) to go out from Babylon and the worldly Egypt, that we should not partake of its stress and strife which the Lord would bring upon them. Out of all this we should learn that all which is not united with our God and Christ is nothing else than the horror which we should avoid and flee.[20]

This separation was a spiritual rather than a geographical matter, although in the generations of persecution and oppression the Anabaptists/Mennonites frequently followed the frontier to realize it.

Infant baptism, the stronghold of territorial Christianity, was repudiated and believers' baptism instituted.

> The present world with its infant baptism is a shocking creation of men without God's word or command, a trickery to the simple and an insidious spot on all Christianity, an arch-knavish cover of all godless; for in the whole Scriptures one cannot produce one single text to defend it.[21]

Baptism is properly a sign of the Covenant of God with His People.

> To this the Lord said: I have elected you from the world. Therefore despise the world. Thereby he could clearly recognize that there was a wide difference between God's children and the children of the world.[22]

Within this Covenant an ethic and a witness were to be completed: the individual who accepted baptism put himself under the admonition and exhortation of the brethren. He was a member of that community which controlled both the Key of David (the true understanding of the Scriptures) and the Keys of Peter (releasing and binding into salvation). That this is a "high" doctrine of the Church, and no marginal sectarianism, is self-evident.

Within the Church the rescued individual was healed, so far as possible, of the marks of his fallen condition. As the beast was turned into a prince by creative Love, the believer was made new in the Second Adam. He became a Man in the full sense of the word. "Without community and without transcendence man is no longer man."[23] He learned, moreover, the disciplines of that ethics which is *Koinonia* ethics — the root of all true Christian ethics.[24] For Christian empathy is learned in faith and perfected in discipline. As a Portuguese philosopher has said of our natural responses: "One endures with patience the pain in the other fellow's stomach." Yet it is the peculiar social genius of Christianity to reform and redirect our natural impulses.

In Him who bore our sorrows and alienations, who saves us from isolation, we are constrained to the sharing of burdens in the practice of brotherhood-love. This can afford a very practical security as well as concern an eternal security. Evidence may be found, for example, in the Department of Agriculture studies of Lancaster County, Pennsylvania, or in this sociologist's study of the Hutterites during the 1930's:

> Without aid or relief, public or private, Hutterites in South Dakota have remained solvent tax-payers in a state in which one-third of the population has been on relief, in which seventy-five per cent of the banks have failed, and in which taxes have become delinquent on approximately one-third of the taxable land.[25]

This practical security is a by-product, however, or — if one prefers — a reward of righteousness. The original concern was to be true to the Lord's will, to obey the Comforter and the Spirit whom He had sent, to execute spiritual government as described in the New Testament.

Community and Communion

The emphasis on community is seen and experienced also in the doctrine of the Lord's Supper, which was reinstituted as a simple observance. In contrast with the ceremonial emphasis, the Anabaptists accented the centrality of the sharing experience. As opposed, for instance, to the Jesuit doctrine of the Mass, in the Free Churches the participants are the locus of the divine act. In the high sacramental tradition, the emphasis is placed upon the great spectacle of the sacrifice upon the altar; the rite is accredited with the objective merit and validity without reference to the time and place or immediate instrument of operation. When the priest celebrates the Mass, even though no other persons may be present at that hour, the devout believe that God is truly present and offered up; if they are present, their experience is that of adoration.

The locus of authority in Free Churches is different. It is not, as sometimes argued, in the individual conscience apart, which has a constant tendency to warp along the lines of individual self-interest. The locus is in the authority of the Holy Spirit in the midst of the covenantal people. Sometimes this means, in practice, "the Spirit of Truth" revealing Himself in the congregation; sometimes, as in episcopal or presbyterial systems, the fellowship which crosses generations is underlined more vigorously. But in either case the principle is the same. And the consequence of the common shared priesthood is that without a believing people no rites or institutions are valid. The first dogma of the Church was and is brotherhood, confessed and experienced, and anteceding all dogmatic formulae or organizational patterns.[26] It is one of the present ironies that precisely at the moment when the Benedictine reform, with the Table of the Lord central to worship, is attracting attention in Catholic circles, some Protestant bodies in search of a liturgy should be adopting an architecture and worship which is ideal for spectators but destructive of community.[27] For Free Churches aware of their heritage, the sharing at the Last Supper is a symbol of an all-controlling way of life.

The Meaning of Consensus

Unfortunate is the way in which discussions of discipline tend to concentrate on minor taboos, which are also chiefly transferred from our culture; more serious is the misapprehension that discipline concentrates attention exclusively on "the lesser excommunication" (barring from the Lord's Table) and "the greater excommunication" (expulsion from the fellowship, the ban). For discipline was and is intended to be a positive testimony, a purposeful program, an arming of the Church for performing her mission in the world. In this, as in other matters, we can often learn from the younger churches; these are, in so many ways, nearer to the churches pastored by Paul than to the more thoroughly established churches of contemporary Christendom.

It was not unusual, for instance, in the earlier Chinese church conferences for someone to arise after a period of difficulty and impasse and say: "Mr. Chairman: I suggest that we are not doing very well, and propose that Mr. — act as

Chairman for a while." This highlights the essential point: not personal prestige, but the achievement of a consensus under the guidance of the Holy Spirit. The more simple form of "talking it up," with a minimum of parliamentary procedure, is still followed by the Hutterites and other residual Free Church communities. The preparation is more important than the actual vote. Sometimes the decision takes years of discussion and seeking for guidance; but the usual practice moves with more dispatch. A Hutterite minister told Lee Emerson Deets:

> I put questions to the members. If anybody is against it, he is to say so. They talk it up in small groups. If the (whole) group gets quiet, then it means "yes." I can tell by the quietness whether they are for it.[28]

The Free Churches are not, it is clear, "free" in structure or opinion; theirs is a real discipline and order which emerges among the members, and is not dictated from above either by prince or by hierarchy. They are resistant to outside interference. They are also suspicious of any who wish to be heard and followed but will not submit themselves to the group. When David Joris appeared at a conference in Strassburg (June, 1538) to win the remaining followers of Melchior Hofmann to his own cause, one of them responded:

> I cannot believe you without further proof. We are ready to learn, but so many of these spirits have come to us with impressive words, and have proclaimed themselves as the Second Sign, the Angel of the Apocalypse, Elijah and Enoch — such as Hans von Rattenburch, Heinrich Schoenmaker, Cloes Elser, Jan Battenburg, the Greek from Macedonia [Melchoir Rinck] and women, whom we have seen and heard ourselves. You claim to speak through the Holy Spirit. Shall we believe you to have been sent? If I came to you and asserted that I spoke through the Spirit, would you believe me?

David Joris could only answer:

> I would let the evidence be given. That is my answer. If you will believe me, I will speak; but if you consider

me from the start to be coming from the Devil, how can I talk with you.[29]

By 1535 the time of the chiliastic prophets was running out in the radical sixteenth-century groups, and the day was at hand when Pilgram Marpeck and the elders would break fellowship with even a spiritualizing millennialist such as Schwenckfeld; they wanted to know nothing of individual inspiration, whether quasi-revolutionary or quietist. The true Christian participated in the life of the community, and was obedient to Him who governed it. Opposition to "mere outward forms," such as produced in Paracelsus[30] and John Perrot[31] a teaching on the unneedfulness of going to church, was furthest from their thoughts. The True Church had integrity and discipline; what was unique in their approach was the way in which that discipline was attained. In contrast to monarchial or hierarchical systems of church government, it was attained by a process which we would today call "democratic" participation.

The attainment of a consensus, and the style of church order and ethic which rested upon it, was the classical Free Church contribution to church government. Those incidents where individuals were, for heresy or immorality, after repeated admonitions excluded from the brotherhood, were painful if necessary by-products. As was said in the Bern Disputation,

> . . . those who lay hold of the Gospel, stand away from error and raise up a Christian life, they are true Christians, have the power to give commandment.[32]

When Schwenckfeld wrote in opposition to the toughness of their approach, it was against him that

> Pilgram Marpeck wrote his great polemic writing in 1542, this most thorough and most profound debate of Anabaptism with all those who wanted to look at Christianity only from the pleasant and friendly side.

They said of the spiritualizer who objected to the ban, that he taught

> only the inward experience and the transfigured, glorified, unsuffering Christ in Heaven, and not the suffering one on Earth; yea, he teaches only the Word of his glory and splendor, and not of his cross and affliction as he bore it before his transfiguration and ascension and as it is still today fitting for his unglorified body to bear.[33]

There was none of the romance of a St. Francis in their willingness to bear the rigorous consequences of their faith; neither was their mood lugubrious. They accepted the necessary consequences of a hardheaded faith, whether it was in obedience to a church discipline which put bounds to individual spontaneity, or in suffering the outrages inflicted by the persecutors. In judging them, the intellectual nobleman Schwenckfeld "always maintained that the Anabaptists lacked the requisite degree of intellectual fitness to prove their propositions."[34] We may imagine that this type of intellectual snobbishness, which compares rather strikingly with criticisms of Billy Graham recently published in the *Episcopal Church News* by J. V. Langmead Casserley,[35] did not disturb the Anabaptists very much. They were willing to "prove their propositions" with their blood.

The early Free Churchmen might have escaped persecution by taking the attitude of those pre-pietist brethren of the sixteenth century who accepted conventicle status for their groups. There were such people. When a group of the *Stille* were brought to court in 1557, and asked why they attended the services of the established church, they replied:

> We all owe this duty in our churches, where the true teaching is, and where idolatry has been done away, and even to God himself, so that we help maintain the Christian public worship, come to church with our children and families and avoid unseemly divisions, so far as possible to us. For Paul says thereto: There shall be no divisions among you. See Psalm 122: You shall wish Jerusalem well; and whoever loves the Church, to him will God give health and prosperity, etc. And this faithful maintenance of the Christian public worship earnestly commanded in the 3rd Commandment: Observe the Sabbath Day.[36]

The Anabaptists did not have, however, so amiable an attitude toward the state churches which had abandoned the disciplines of Christian brotherhood; nor did they have so limited a view of the meaning of their own faith. They loved to fellowship; moreover, they had learned a way in which Christians might live and share a common life which was poles apart from religion as a cultural institution.

Community as the Central Discipline

It is interesting in this connection that one of the leading interpreters of the rift between Christ and culture in our own time, Karl Barth, should have in recent writings been brought to question infant baptism, to appeal to the tradition of the seventeenth-century Free Churches as against the hierarchies ruled by professionals, and to center on the congregation as the real locus of Christian government.

> Against the papal, but also against the episcopal and presbyterian/synodal concept stands the fundamental fact that they do not serve but actually hinder the readiness, the openness, the freedom of the congregation for the Word of God and the reformation of the Church.[37]

The estrangement between Christ and culture is not, of course, a distance in time between the eighteenth and the twentieth century. In this regard the experience of the Quakers with "plain clothing," which became *peculiar* clothing, is relevant. To quote the excellent study of Amelia Mott Gummere:

> The dress of the Quaker, when he first arose, was in cut and fashion simply the dress of everybody, with all extravagances left off.
>
> The gentleman of fashion in 1695 wore his hair long under a broad plumed hat. The jeweled sword at his side dangled from an embroidered scarf; enormous coat cuffs concealed his hands, when they were not thrust into a large muff. The large bordered hat was turned up at three sides, and until 1710 kept the adornment of plumes. . . . Both sexes wore small looking-glasses. Men even wore them in their hats.

She quotes Margaret Fell's warning of as early as 1698:

> Legal ceremonies are far from Gospel freedom; let us beware of being guilty or having a hand in ordering or contriving what is contrary to Gospel freedom; for the Apostles would not have domination over their faith, but be helpers of their faith. It is a dangerous thing to lead young Friends much into the observation of outward things, which may easily be done, for they can soon get into an outward garb to be all alike outwardly, but this will not make them true Christians.[38]

It is more fitting for a member to discuss this matter in detail among the "plain clothes" people. A nonmember may perhaps be allowed to raise the prior question: To what degree, and in what form, are simple and plain living a part of the Christian witness? This is a question for all the churches, which might indeed learn a good deal from each other. We have been assured repeatedly in recent years that it is of major importance on the mission field that those sent out share the standard of living of those whom they serve.[39] Those Christians who adopted the national average standard of living some years ago, in England, were concerned to break the identification of Christianity with privileged groups in the population, and implement the mission to the poor and the outcasts.

We return to the basic issue of discipline. It is not based on physical separation so much as spiritual separation. The Church does not accent discipline for its own sake, but because it is the Lord's will that his people be armed as well as possible for the spiritual battle. The Church is "cut loose from the world," but she does not abandon it; rather, "putting on the whole armor of God" she sends her missioners forth to preach the Gospel to every creature.

VII. The Free Churches and Ecumenics

> The church exists exists by mission just as a fire exists by burning.
>
> — Emil Brunner

The Free Churches the First Missionary Churches

No Christian discipline is a more integral part of the Free Church heritage, since the earliest days, than the mission to preach, to heal, to free. The territorial establishments did not come to missionary action until the rise of pietism on the Continent and the Evangelical Awakening in the British Isles led to the organization of missionary societies for that special purpose. The Anabaptists of the sixteenth century were mission-minded at a time when both Roman Catholics and state church Protestants saw nothing illogical in dividing up Christendom by political agreement. And that "world-mindedness" was not among special groups who organized themselves to effect a special purpose; it existed throughout the entire membership. Whereas the Reformers maintained that the Great Commission had exhausted its claim during the age of the Apostles, the Anabaptists/Mennonites asserted that it was still in force for every baptized believer.

The conviction that the whole earth should be brought to Christ produced Anabaptist martyrs in the most distant capitals of Europe at a time when the scholasticism of the third generation of the Reformers was debating the use of vowel points in "the language that God spoke" (Hebrew). It is hard to avoid the remark, remembering the savage persecution of these same missioners, that the Anabaptists were more concerned about *what* He said than the particular form of utterance. But the peculiar problems of Biblicism have never been indigenous to Anabaptism; they had a key to unlock and make intelligible the Scriptures in the life and spirit of the community itself. In the life of the Christian community, properly ordered and governed by the Holy Spirit, a continuing and renewing tradition is possible which escapes the cultural limits of Biblicism, legalism, or credalism. True Anabaptists have never been fundamentalists.

Of the problem of missions in the sixteenth century, James Thayer Addison has written:

> For nearly two centuries the Churches of the Reformation were almost destitute of any sense of missionary vocation. The foremost leaders — men like Luther, Melanchthon, Bucer, Zwingli, and Calvin — displayed neither missionary vision nor missionary spirit. While conceding in theory the universality of Christianity, they never recognized it as a call to the Church of their day. Indeed some of them even interpreted "Go ye into all the world" as a command already executed in the past and now no longer operative. And the very few thinkers who rejected this deadening view remained without influence.[1]

The influence of the Free Churches, however, was to be felt in due time. The fact that those of the direct line of the Anabaptists have constantly been forced over the generations to migrate to the frontier, where an agrarian exclusiveness for a time crippled the essentially missionary character of their faith,[2] has obscured the major contribution of the Anabaptist pioneers to missionary theory and practice. It is not only in the Anabaptist/Mennonite tradition that persecution has produced a psychology of withdrawal in place of the glorious proclamation that in Christ all things are made new. Reinhold Niebuhr has written of a certain type of contemporary European religious thought, which, having held the fortress of the faith against unbelief and oppression during the Nazi time, now finds difficulty in articulating a comprehensive Christian apologetic:

> Yesterday they discovered that the church may be an ark in which to survive a flood. Today they seem so en-

> amored of this special function of the church that they have decided to turn the Ark into a home on Mount Ararat and live it in perpetually.[3]

Permanent withdrawal, however, is no true function of the Free Church view of the Church Militant; where such withdrawal has existed it has been a product of cultural or political forces rather than a basic conviction.

It has been said that the escutcheon of one large American denomination consists of "a Question Mark rampant, with three Bishops dormant." The passion for winning the world to Christ can be lost in various ways, most of which are forms of accommodation to dominant cultural patterns or forces. This can have its "idealistic" aspects, as when the dean of a certain school of theology remarked in the writer's presence during a discussion of the doctrine of the Christian hope that he thought the churches would do well to give up all their creeds and confessions, which simply divide the world, and take as their testimony the Declaration on Human Rights of the United Nations! Presumably a Biblical God who was too "jealous" to take his assigned niche among the pagan gods of the Roman pantheon would now, in this enlightened twentieth (nineteenth?) century move over to his proper place in a congress of world religions. Perhaps the time has come when an old-fashioned God will give up His foolishness and affirm the wisdom of men. But as long as there are those who know Jesus the Christ, there will be those who speak of Him and declare abroad what they have seen done in His name.

> Being confident of this very thing, that he which hath begun a good work in you will perform it until the day of Jesus Christ. (Phil. 1:3-6)

The Book of the World was an impossible concept when it infatuated Sebastian Franck in the sixteenth century; it is no more fruitful in the hands of contemporary spiritualizers. The concept of the future things is the key which unlocks history. It rests on the faith that He is faithful who has promised.

The Anabaptist churches were missionary churches. Long before the battle cry of the Student Volunteer Movement was heard, they taught that every believing Christian should either go to the field or support those who did. The Hutterite chronicles are full of instances where the families of the missioners were provided for by the community. Menno Simons was able to write, as years of danger and fugitive missionizing went by without fixed salary or post, that he had yet "to see the righteous forsaken, or his seed begging bread" (Psalm 37:25). Some years ago an American writer, attempting to formulate the concepts "church" and "sect" along lines more intelligible sociologically than theologically, wrote:

> *A sect, sociologically speaking, is any religious group which makes no claim to universality and the bond of union between whose members is free and voluntary in character.* The logical implication of particularism and voluntarism are *separation* and an *ascetic ethics.*[4]

The Free Church pioneers, like their spiritual children, qualify in certain respects within the above definition. Yet at the key point they do not: they claim the universality of their church, and its coming triumph, in the fullness of time. They believed the Biblical teaching that God is using his elect to gather all peoples. They clearly repudiated the chiliasm of such prophets as Augustin Bader and Johann Batenburg; but they looked toward the time when the Lord should come again with power, and judge the quick and the dead. Theirs was no marginal critique of the standing order in Christendom, no conventicle program for the enrichment of the established churches. They counted themselves spiritual children of the Covenant of Abraham, with the very meaning of history itself embodied in their congregations. Their view of the Church was a "high" view; their understanding of its universality was rich and full.

The Anabaptist hope was not in the world and its natural development, but in what God intended for the world. At Edinburgh in 1910 a piercing question was asked, which they would readily have understood:

> Shall we ever recover the daring optimism of the early days, until we have more deeply understood the pessimism out of which it sprang? Are we not in danger of forgetting the radical supernaturalism of Christianity.[5]

A world which thinks more highly of itself than it ought, a world which crucified the Best Man who ever lived — and has continued to deny Him — is nevertheless a world in which the devil is loose by sufferance, and over which God's hovering providence is never absent. It is a world of whose ambivalence between extreme relativism and extreme absolutism Hendrik Kraemer wrote:

> Nothing can demonstrate more clearly that *the Christian Church, religiously speaking, in the West as well as the East, is standing in a pagan, non-Christian world, and has again to consider the whole world its mission field, not in the rhetorical but in the literal sense of the word.*[6]

It is a world on which T. S. Eliot commented: "Great Britain is neither pagan nor Christian: it tolerates the Christian way of life."[7] When Georg Blaurock was expelled by the town authorities for missionary activity, he said that he wouldn't leave Zurich territory but would rather die. "For the earth is the Lord's!" (Psalm 24:1)

The Eschatological Note

The consciousness of living before the end is not limited in our time to Jehovah's Witnesses or other small groups whom the large church bodies consider unnecessarily excitable. In fact the marvel of the age is rather the survival of so much of the nineteenth-century mood and type. As one Dutch resister wrote of the break-up of the old order before Nazism:

> We thought we were walking on a marble floor — it has shown itself a crumbling sheet of ice . . . then the thaw set in — and now the dark waters yawn below.[8]

America, with its yet intact society, is perhaps less aware

of the crisis of culture than certain European churches who have experienced the demonic nihilism in their own bodies, and are now directly confronted by an anti-Christian "cosmism" of gigantic proportions. Yet those of our citizens whose daily decisions deal with life and death often have a more sensitive awareness of the depths of the human predicament than many of the professionals to whom the people look in vain for the Biblical Word. The first atom bomb was exploded in Almagordo; the man who set it off (Henrique Berbal) is now a monk in Spain. The man who piloted the plane from which fire was hurled on Hiroshima (Robert Lewis) is now a Trappist. While sin is still a dirty word to large groups of speculative philosophers and supposed theologians, the technicians and scientists — to quote one of their foremost personalities, Harold Urey — "have known sin."

The proclamation of the eschatological dimension is not, as a superficial intellectual would have it, the result of pernicious influence from a Europe which has suffered two world wars and a depression. Those religious thinkers who have managed to escape the meaning of the history of the last decades would, like Antaeus, grow stronger by getting their feet back on the ground. At a time when infatuation with the merely contemporary has clouded so much thinking, even in our seminaries, we do well to reflect with that great ecumenical leader, Georges Florovsky, on the richness and relevance of our Christian heritage:

> The fathers were wrestling with existing essential problems, with those revelations of the eternal issues which were described and recorded in Holy Writ. I would risk the suggestion that St. Athanasius and St. Augustine are much more up to date than many of our theological contemporaries.[9]

Compared with the fathers, much of contemporary Christian philosophical writing is puerile and uninteresting. The Anabaptists did not repudiate the Church fathers, but they looked first to Holy Writ. And the eschatological note ran like a red thread through the fabric of their teaching.

return to basics "better times"

Hope and Discipline Belong Together

The significant fact is that eschatology and discipline rise and fall together. The loss of discipline in the nineteenth-century churches of Europe paralleled the loss of confidence in the Christian future. And here, again, the secular religions have taken over and capitalized on a neglected element in the Christian faith. Many students of Communism have commented that a major strength of the movement, even among those unwillingly taken captive, is precisely its absolute confidence in the historical inevitability of the revolution and millennium to come. Contemporary totalitarianism is something more than a new manifestation of recurring despotism: *it has an eschatology.*

> Montesquieu remarks that religion works as a check in despotic regimes which do not have any institutional or traditional checks against the arbitrary actions of the despot. An essential feature of totalitarianism consists in the disappearance of this factual, though neither legal nor institutional limiting power of religious habits and customs. On the contrary, energies and forces which formerly had their outlet and expression in religion, limiting the old despotic ruler, are now driving forces behind and in the new despotic regimes of the 20th century. The totalitarian ideologies replace and supersede religion.
>
> Therefore it may be said that the various forms of totalitarianism — Nazism and Soviet Communism — are politico-social secularized religions, characteristic of our epoch. The totalitarian movements and their power replace God and religious institutions such as the Church; the leaders are deified; the public mass-meetings are regarded and celebrated as sacred actions; the history of the movement becomes a holy history of the advance of salvation, which the enemies and betrayers try to prevent in the same way as the devil tries to undermine and destroy the work of those who are in the service of the City of God.[10]

The scandal of Christendom is not alone that the churches are weak in the face of dynamic anti-Christian ideologies; it is that through faithlessness and relaxation they have created a loss of Hope, into which the pseudo-religions rushed with their answers. The encounter of the Christian Church with the surviving totalitarians is a *total* encounter, not a confrontation where we can pick and choose.

> Some Christian apologists would say that Marxism fails to give us an adequate account of personality, or of sin, or of morality, or of death. . . . But my own conviction is that, in this matter as in every other, it is far better that Christianity should take its own standing-ground and argue from its own starting-point. And that starting point is the history of Israel and the events to which the Apostolic preaching and the Church both testify. For Christianity does not rest upon an empirical (scientific) investigation of the nature of the world, any more than it rests upon philosophic speculation about the nature of God. Christianity rests upon the historic fact of Christ, upon the prophetic witness which testified of Him and upon the apostolic witness in which the meaning of His Coming is set forth.[11]

The first Christians — not those who repeated his words and compared his ideas with those of other Jewish teachers, but the men who looked at Jesus and beheld the Christ of God — went out and told of Him who was the pivot of history.

"World-Mindedness" in the Free Churches

As the Anabaptist/Mennonite missioners were convinced that they spoke of Him from whom all human history takes its meaning, so were they persuaded that the whole world must hear of it. They believed that they were living again, as members of a restored Church, in the time of apostolic power and the fulfillment of promises. Georg Zaunring went through the land "to gather the Lord's sheep" and "to fish for men."[12] Paul Glock wrote in 1563:

> Blessed is the man whom the Lord when he comes finds waking. At first He speaks of cutting loose; by this we are to understand that we must wander. . . . Also we are to understand by cutting loose that we shall lift up our

> countenance and thoughts to the heavenly things, that the world spot us not.[13]

The mood of great expectation appeared later in the Free Church tradition in the slogan, "Dare great things for God!" The itineraries of the traveling Friends of the seventeenth century covered the known world:

> Florence, Mantua, Palatine, Tuscany, Italy, Rome, Turkey, Jerusalem, France, Geneva, Norway, Barbados, Antigua, Jamaica, Surinam, Newfoundland.[14]

There was no tribe too remote, no people too primitive or despised, no race or color so contemptible as to be unworthy of the news of the astonishing blessings God had prepared for them through His son Jesus Christ. In the Free Church of the sixteenth and seventeenth centuries there was realized that concept of the whole Church as a missionary people, which has in the last century and a half produced such marvelous results in spreading the faith to the uttermost reaches of the earth.

"Integral" Christianity

The bringing of the whole world under the Lord's dominion is a universal — a catholic, an ecumenical — view of the Biblical hope. The hope has two dimensions: geographical ("world-mindedness") and what has here been called "integral" (i.e., commanding all of life). By "integral" Christianity is meant neither that pious individualism which denies that certain areas of this pilgrim life come under the impact of the Gospel (*de novo* fundamentalism), nor that well-meaning type of liberalism which is always talking over the heads of the congregations to all intelligent and progressive citizens willing to hear. "Integral" is used, for lack of a better term, to anchor all such discussions to the Church and her mission. It implies a view of the Church in which the first person singular — both that of the religious anarchism of a certain style of stereotyped fundamentalist convert, and that of the frivolous eclecticism of a certain type of enlightened spiritualizer — is reduced to proper perspective. It implies a "high" doctrine of the Church and her mission, in which sanitary regulations in Cleveland, milk for Hottentots, and unintimidated distribution of Bibles in Colombia all come under the impress of the Divine Word. "For God will bring every work into judgment . . ." (Eccles. 12:14a).

"Integral" Christianity implies above all that the People of God shall not pretend to a program of action which is beyond its disciplined capacities, that it shall not declare any new idea or plan to the world until it has made incarnate the consequences thereof within its own ranks. A Church of integrity, in short, will not moralize to the world about the evils of discrimination and racialism until it admits to membership and the communion table all qualified persons regardless of race or color; it will not talk about a materialistic success philosophy in the world while it allows a callow type of careerism in its pulpits; it will not prate about corruption in politics at the time it holds its membership open to those same corrupt politicians. It will begin and carry through its renewing and redeeming mission with self-examination, internal discipline, and obedience to the governance of the Ruler of the Church.

The Sin of Dividedness Being Overcome

Of all the blemishes which mar the countenance of the Universal Church none is more serious than its dividedness. For this reason the Anabaptists of the sixteenth century, like many of their spiritual children, wanted to be known only as "Christians" or "Brethren." They were not eager founders of new churches; they were simply faithful to their vision of "the one holy catholic Church." That they eventually were succeeded by denominations was not their intention; it was because the existing bodies rejected their counsel and refused to hear their testimony.

The ecumenical movement is primarily a product of the experience of the churches in the foreign missions field. Because the Federal Council of Churches arose in the period, and to a marked degree under the impress, of the Social Gospel in America,[15] we are apt to forget this important fact about the history of those consultations which led up to the founding of the World Council of Churches at Amsterdam in 1948. The Federal Council, like the "Social Creed of the Churches" and the Religious Education Association, grew out of that era in the American churches of progressive social thought, featured by the great Social Christianity Congresses of the Evangelical Alliance (1887, 1889, 1893) which brought together 12,000 to 15,000 delegates. It was a period characterized by the spirit and mind of Sheldon's *In His Steps,* of which 23,000,000 copies were sold, and Stead's *If Christ Came to Chicago,* a bestseller of several hundred thousand copies. The "Brotherhood of the Kingdom" which gathered about Walter Rauschenbusch (1861-1918) was, nevertheless, marked by evangelical faith and discipline as well as social optimism. It is in the second and third generation that the hybrid goes to seed, as in the total lack of theological mooring revealed in the writings of Henry F. Ward or in the drifting of the Methodist Federation for Social Action. The Federal Council, in the meantime, combined with other interdenominational agencies in the National Council of the Churches of Christ in America, has under a wiser leadership matured in a more Church-centered strategy.

The first of the great Ecumenical Councils was the 1910 World Missionary Conference in Edinburgh. The concern from the beginning was that which Bishop Azariah expressed at Lausanne (1927):

> Unity may be theoretically a desirable ideal in Europe and America, but it is vital to the life of the Church in the mission field. The divisions of Christendom may be a source of weakness in Christian countries, but in non-Christian lands they are a sin and a scandal.[16]

The concern was from the beginning precisely where it belongs: with the shaping of an effective testimony to the one Lord, one faith, one baptism, which are the common confession of all who name His Name.

The progress made in interchurch understanding has

never been accomplished through harmonism or through spiritualizing of problems of order and discipline. The advances in understanding and co-operative effort, which have led even some secular historians to term the ecumenical movement the "greatest event of the twentieth century," have been achieved through common prayer, common worship, joint study, and open discussion. A person who has participated in one or more such international and interchurch sessions can testify fairly that the practice is one of decision through consensus, and that those matters which cannot be readily disposed of are "talked up" over years and even generations. This being the case, it seems to me that men of the Free Churches can and should join in heartily — so long as such procedures are observed and the guidance of the Holy Spirit is looked to as the one effective pillar of fire which can lead us out of our dead ends of divided creed and divided order.

Fellowship with Heroes

Such fraternity with the men of the old establishments who also confess His name is today possible, although in former generations impossible, not only because they have given up coercion as a means of evangelization (and are no longer establishments in the old sense of the term), but because they are in fact as ready to listen to His word in the congregations as are we. Let us quote the testimonies of heroes of spiritual resistance.

Peter Yorck von Wartenburg:

> The decisive factor which brings together all these questions is the totalitarian claim of the State on the individual which forces him to renounce his moral and religious obligation to God.[17]

Dietrich Bonhoeffer:

> If we claim to be Christians there is no room for expediency. Hitler is Anti-Christ, therefore we must go on with our work and eliminate him whether he be successful or not.[18]

The men of the Barmen Synod, who re-affirmed the radical consequences of Biblical religion in the fact of a wicked dictator, were representing us. Of special meaning to Free Churchmen is the fact that they were resisting improper political interference in the Church.

> This so-called national synod of Berlin and its decisions and deliberations are all invalid according to principles of ecclesiastical law. Whoever complies is (therefore) breaking the constitution and violating the laws of the Church.
>
> The Reich government despises the fundamentals of law and justice. . . . It is devoid of the brotherly love made obligatory by the Holy Scriptures. Therefore it forsakes the fundamentals of the Reformation Church built upon the Gospel. . . . He who consciously breaks laws which it is his personal duty to defend has foregone the right to expect obedience. Obedience to this church government is disobedience to God.[19]

With the spread of the Third Reich, the churches of the Netherlands and Norway faced also a basic question of existence, and their integrity asserted itself. A Dutch Pastoral Letter of Eight Articles was circulated in the autumn of 1943, and it ran along Biblical lines:

> The first and decisive thing which has to be said about the relationship between the Christian faith and National Socialism is this: National Socialism confesses a god other than the God of the Holy Scriptures; it seeks a salvation other than the Salvation through Jesus Christ, and it takes practical form in a life of faith which is the absolute *opposite* of the life born from faith in Jesus Christ through the Holy Spirit.[20]

Significantly, the Eighth Article of the Pastoral dealt with questions of church discipline: refusing communion and church marriage to members of the Dutch Nazi Party, refusing Christian burial to those who enlisted and died fighting for Hitler on the Eastern Front, dealing with the life of the congregations in loving care and wise admonition. From the Netherlands we receive the testimony of a young Christian martyr who died in a concentration camp. An official high in The Hague and instructed to enforce the edicts against the Jews, he assembled his colleagues in July, 1940, and addressed them as follows:

> I find it necessary, my dear colleagues, to explain to you why some days ago I handed in my resignation from the position of General Secretary. I learnt at that moment that the "Aryan paragraph" was soon to be introduced. In consequence it will in future be necessary at every staff nomination to enquire whether the person in question is of Jewish ancestry. For this reason I am forced to hand in my resignation. For, as a confessing Christian, and as a Dutchman, I could not ask anyone this question. It is against the deepest foundations of our faith in Jesus Christ, in whom God reveals Himself to all men and before whom all men are equal, to prefer one man to another because he belongs to a certain race or a certain nationality. And more than that: the fact that the Jewish people is declared to be inferior contradicts the Word of God, for it has pleased God in his marvelous and unfathomable mercy, to give redemption to all peoples and races through Jesus Christ who came from the midst of the Jewish people. Every rejection of the Jewish people is therefore a rejection of Jesus Christ.
>
> And finally I know through faith that, above all fighting and strife and struggle, the Gospel of Jesus Christ speaks personally in the same way to every human being of whatever race and nation, and therefore I cannot, holding this faith, distinguish between friend or enemy, whether he be Dutch, German or Jew. For all need the mercy and forgiveness of Jesus Christ, every human being needs it, as I myself also can only live and die through grace.
>
> What my future will be I know as little as any one of you can know, but no one need be troubled for this reason, because I know that when my strength gives way I may expect all strength from Him who does not leave man even in his greatest need.
>
> Therefore I wish to close by reading to you the

> 23rd Psalm in which many centuries ago the Jewish seer gave voice to his unshakeable faith in God.[21]

If we do not have fellowship with this man, if we do not raise our voices in prayer for all Christians similarly placed, it is we who are unworthy — and not the one who received from his fathers another teaching on the nature of the church order.

Free Churchmen have every reason to rejoice for and pray with Reinold von Thadden-Trieglaff, President of the Kirchentag, as his growing movement of laymen takes the Church back to the people. And this is not alone because the experience out of which it grew was a little fellowship of Lutheran, Baptist, Mennonite and Roman Catholic laymen in a Russian POW camp, who kept their souls alive by common prayer, reading of the Bible, and song.[22] We rejoice in the Evangelist Tung, who in spite of Communist persecution in China refused to forswear our Lord. Of him it was reported:

> In expounding the Genesis story of the serpent Tung Ling Ku accused the government of traveling the crooked way of the snake in its approach to problems and likened the Communist folk dance (two steps forward, one back) to the twisting, rolling motion of a serpent. Speaking of Esau's deal with Jacob he said that some church members were selling their church for a mess of bean soup. He identified the red horse of Revelation as the Red army. He likened the church to the man who went down to Jericho, not daring to occupy his rightful place, and on the way was robbed because of his sin, stripped of his resemblance to the Christian faith. Those who passed along the road, the church leaders, were unable to help him to restore his spiritual welfare, for they were engaged in the affairs of the world.
>
> "These are not the servants of God," he was alleged to have said, "and therefore should be dethroned."[23]

The peculiar form of Tung's theology is incidental. If we are proud of our fellow Christian, Tung Ling Ku, it is not just because in his own way he has refused to bow the knee to Baal, nor because the community of which he was a servant was — until the advent of the Communist People's Democracy — a Free Church in the precise sense of the word; rather it is because we would have fellowship with all who serve or suffer for the Lord Jesus, who lay aside every weight, and sin which clings so closely, and run with patience the race that is set before us (Hebrews 12:1).

Divisive and Unitive Factors in the American Churches

In the American churches, the weight which is upon us is primarily cultural; and nowhere is the effect of outside cultural influence more evident than in our dividedness. A study of the divisions will thoroughly establish the fact that they have not, in most cases, occurred or been maintained because of differences in confession or basic discipline: they are the result of cultural and national and linguistic differences in origin and development. In the words of H. Richard Niebuhr, who laid bare the major causes of our dividedness,

> Denominational Christianity, that is Christianity which surrenders its leadership to the social forces of national and economic life, offers no hope to the divided world. Lacking an integrating ethics, lacking a universal appeal, it continues to follow the fortunes of the world, gaining petty victories in a war it has long lost.[24]

With the emphasis the world likes to place on the existence of 276 different "Protestant" churches in America, it is possible to forget the unitive factor. Of organized religious bodies in America, only thirty-five number over 200,000 members, and together they include 93,000,000 of the 97,-482,611 total numbered in the 1954 census.[25] The whole argument of this paper has been, to be sure, that strength is not in numbers. But strength is, quite directly, in faithfulness to the sometimes forgotten half of the missionary and universal world-view of the Church: that all men may be brought to the feet of Christ *and* that all his servants may be *one.*

A Continuing Restitution

Much is written, from time to time, about a "continuing Reformation." This writer would like to propose a *continuing Restitution.* For the process of redefining and rediscovering the Biblical fellowship is the process of creating it anew. In this discussion all faithful Christians, whatever their diverse theological origins, may participate. It is this restored and catholic Church, obedient in discipline and governed by the Holy Spirit, which can bring to all men who have ears to hear knowledge of His truth and in the world to come life everlasting.

> *O God, the Father of our Lord Jesus Christ, our only Saviour, the Prince of Peace; Give us grace seriously to lay to heart the great dangers we are in by our unhappy divisions. Take away all hatred and prejudice, and whatsoever else may hinder us from godly union and concord: that as there is but one Body and one Spirit, and one home of our calling, one Lord, one Faith, one Baptism, one God and Father of us all, so we may be all of one heart and of one soul, united in one holy bond of truth and peace, of faith and charity and may with one mind and mouth glorify thee; through Jesus Christ our Lord. Amen.* — *The Book of Common Prayer*

Epilogue

If this writing has achieved its purpose, the reader will understand that what is at stake is a certain approach to dealing with specific problems. The democratic way is essentially a problem-solving method, whether used in the political area or in the life of the Church. Our fathers, who were not too struck with their own genius to admit dependence upon One far greater and wiser, were accustomed to refer to Him matters of political import as readily as ecclesiastical. They believed that if a people called on His name with abandon, He would not leave them without guidance. The answer would not be an absolute one — i.e., sufficient for all times and places — but it would be enough to live by. The "discussion method" is a secularized version of this "waiting on the Lord," and when properly understood and practiced it will not stray very far from its original setting.

The forms of political self-government and the Free Church, rightly understood, are historically and presently inextricably bound up together. This is not because both owe allegiance to some speculative "freedom," but rather because both are based on the process of reaching decisions by discussion ⟶ consensus. The man who stands in Christian liberty will, therefore, avoid pat programs as rigorously as he avoids the bastard millennialism which pervades totalitarian systems. Knowing the Comforter, the Spirit of Truth, he will defer to God's time and avoid the pretentiousness of attempting to force Divine sanction on his own calendar and plans.

Candor compels the admission that, by classical standards, our American churches have taken on the character of establishments. They may still flatter themselves that they have escaped any large measure of political control (the *negative* phase of Free Churchmanship), but in terms of theological and ethical discipline (i.e., the disciplined community witness to the working of the Holy Spirit — the *positive* phase of Free Church life), the larger denominations, at least, are establishments. They *believe* what college graduates in America believe, and they *practice* what suburban mores dictate. In the long view, acceptance of status as *social establishments* can be as fatal as *political establishment.*

When will our American churches abandon culture religion and turn again to the Lord? At that moment when the people who bear His Name are tired of easy answers and little godlets, and begin to speak and write and debate and pray — to "wrestle" — with the Angel of the Lord.

When will American democracy recover from its uncertainties, anxieties, hysterics? When as fellow citizens we have ceased to whine and tease God to sanctify *our* ideals and have recovered the practice of the Divine initiative.

Although a few examples have been given throughout, the writer has had no intention to describe programs of reform. He has his own ideas, when the appropriate time comes; there are others. But all are fruitless so long as serious proposals, brought forward "bindingly," are simply regarded as intellectual amusement for jaded religious spectators. If our churches grow discontented in time with their chase after "peace of mind," their "Man Upstairs," their "American religion," then the practice of Christian Community may again take precedence.

Over generations, a republican form of government cannot exist without a network of vigorous and internally disciplined voluntary associations, including churches. And the Church, and the Lord of the Church, will not take up residence where all worship Apollo (appearance) or Baal (production).

"Come, let us reason together, saith the Lord" (Isaiah 1:18).

Footnotes

PREFACE

1. (J.C.B. Mohr, 1931), Tübingen, V, 1915-17.
2. (Random House, 1952), N. Y., pp. 286-327.
3. Dillenberger, John, and Welch, Claude, *Protestant Christianity* (Charles Scribner's Sons, 1954), N. Y., pp. 63ff. See also excellent appraisals in Bainton, Roland H., *The Reformation of the Sixteenth Century* (Beacon Press, 1952), Boston, Chap. V, and Grimm, Harold J., *The Reformation Era* (Macmillan Co., 1954), N. Y., pp. 265-75.
4. Cf. report in LXIX *The Christian Century* (1952) 39:1105. About the same time it was reported that students at the University of Kiel, Germany, were taking over patronage of a memorial to Menno Simons to be erected at Oldesloe near Hamburg. *Religious News Service: Foreign* (8/5/52). Hereafter *RNS.*
5. "Theology in the Ecumenical Age," IV *Theology Today* (1947) 1:19-33, 25-26.
6. Cf. *The Anabaptist View of the Church* (American Society of Church History, 1952), Chicago, *passim.*
7. Private correspondence with E. B., dated 3/8/56.
8. Wedel, Theodore O., *The Coming Great Church* (Macmillan Co., 1945), N. Y., pp. vii, 46.

CHAPTER I. *The Basic Issues, the Threats*

1. Terminology introduced by Robert Friedmann in "Conception of the Anabaptists," IX *Church History* (1940), pp. 341-65.
2. Reported in XXVII *The Lutheran* (1945) 52:4.
3. Bailie, John, *What Is Christian Civilization?* (Charles Scribner's Sons, 1945), N. Y., p. 25.
4. *Ibid.*, p. 41.
5. Henderson, G. D., *The Claims of the Church of Scotland* (Hodder & Stoughton, Ltd., 1951), London, Chap. VIII.
6. Bates, M. Searle, *Religious Liberty: An Inquiry* (International Missionary Council, 1945), N. Y. and London, p. 151.
7. Edited by Joseph I. Parker, 1928, New York.
8. Latourette, Kenneth S., "A Historian Looks Ahead: the Future of Christianity in the Light of its Past," XV *Church History* (1946) 1:3-16, 14.
9. On current developments in Germany see: "Church and Sect (with special reference to Germany)," VI *The Ecumenical Review* (1954) 3:267-75.
10. On this point see "Spiritualizers, Anabaptists, and the Church," XXIX *The Mennonite Quarterly Review* (1955) 1:34-43.
11. The same Roman Catholic Church which bitterly complains of its loss of privileges in Poland and Bohemia is prepared to defend openly the continued suppression of Protestant church work; *RNS:Foreign* (10/13/52). Recent agreements between the Vatican and a National

Communist Poland (Nov./Dec., 1956) reveal that although it is easier for Rome to reach agreement with black totalitarianism than with red, the latter is not impossible.

12. Count the incidence of the first person singular in a representative mystical item such as Gibran's *The Prophet;* or "The Quiet Time," Chap. IV, in Thurman, Howard, *Deep is the Hunger* (Harper & Bros., 1951), N. Y.
13. *A Quaker Mutation* (Pendle Hill Pamphlet No. 7, 1939), Wallingford, Penna., p. 9.
14. *The Anabaptist View of the Church* (American Society of Church History, 1952), Chicago, pp. 13, 35f.
15. Angus, S., *The Religious Quests of the Graeco-Roman World* (Charles Scribner's Sons, 1929), N. Y., p. x.
16. Written before the XX Party Congress in Moscow, 1956!
17. Voegelin, Eric, *The New Science of Politics* (University of Chicago Press, 1952), Chicago; Muehlenfeld, Hans, *Politik ohne Wunschbilder* (Verlag von R. Oldenburg, 1952), Muenchen.
18. Brinton, Crane, *The Shaping of the Modern Mind* (New American Library, 1953), N. Y., p. 19.
19. Black, Matthew, "The Covenant of People," LVII *The Expository Times* (1946) 10:277-78; George, A. Raymond, "The Doctrine of the Church," LVIII *The Expository Times* (1947) 12:312-16. The Christian Church is the center of experience; the internal ethic is the important question; cf. Manson, T. W., "The Unity of the New Testament: New Testament Ethics," LVIII *The Expository Times* (1947) 11:284-87.
20. Cf. discussion in Wright, G. Ernest, *The Old Testament Against Its Environment* (S.C.M. Press, Ltd., 1950), London, Chap. II, section 3.
21. Filson, Floyd V., *The New Testament Against Its Environment* (S.C.M. Press, Ltd., 1950), London, p. 77. The new thing which entered was fellowship, symbolized by the loaf, with religious efficacy expressed in knowledge of the Truth demonstrated by mighty works. Cf. Scott, C. A. Anderson, "What Happened at Pentecost," in Streeter, B. H., ed., *The Spirit* (Macmillan Co., 1921), London, p. 132.
22. Wedel, Theodore O., *The Coming Great Church* (Macmillan Co., 1945), N. Y., p. 60. The archeologists advise us that the first places of meetings were House-churches; note the Yale excavations as Dura-Europos. The family, a primary social unit, was central; the church of both Old and New Testaments is a Covenant of Families.
23. *The Biblical Doctrine of Election* (Lutterworth Press, 1950), London, p. 174.
24. Cf. Bigelmair, Andreas, *Die Beteiligung der Christen am oeffentlichen Leben in vorconstantinischer Zeit* (J. J. Lentner'sche Buchh., 1902), Muenchen, pp. 23-24.
25. Richardson, Cyril, "Orders and the Proposed Concordat," CLIII *The Churchman* (1939) 16:14-16, 17:14-15.

CHAPTER II. *How the Free Church Emerged*

1. See Mirbt, Carl, *Quellen zur Geschichte des Papsttums und des Römischen Katholizismus* (J.C.B. Mohr, 1934), Tübingen, No. 372.
2. Woodward, E. L., *Christianity and Nationalism in the Later Roman*

Empire (Longmans, Green & Co., 1916), London, p. vi. On the Donatists as a Punic-speaking movement, over against the Latin-speaking power drive, see pp. 5f.

3. Quoted in Lecler, Joseph, *The Two Sovereignties* (Philosophical Library, 1952), N. Y., p. 101.
4. Figgis, John Neville, *The Political Aspects of S. Augustine's 'City of God'* (Longmans, Green and Co., 1921), London, p. 86.
5. Cf. Werdermann, Th., "Calvins Lehre von der Kirche in ihrer geschichtlichen Entwicklung," in *Calvinstudien* (Rudolph Haupt, 1909), Leipzig, pp. 281ff.
6. Lindsay, Thomas M., *A History of the Reformation* (Charles Scribner's Sons, 1941), N. Y. Reprint of 1907 edition. II, 112, footnote 3.
7. Weisz, Leo, *Leo Jud: Ulrich Zwingli's Kampfgenosse (1482-1542)* (Zwingli Verlag, 1942), Zurich, pp. 91ff, 101f.
8. Hartmann, Julius, *Johannes Brenz: Leben und ausgewaehlte Schriften* (R. L. Friderichs, 1862), Elberfeld, p. 106.
9. Acton, John Emerich Edward Dahlberg, *Essays on Freedom and Power* (Beacon Press, 1948), Boston, edited by Gertrude Himmelfarb, Chap. IV.
10. Verduin, Leonard, "On Detesting Anabaptists," *The Calvin Forum* (April, 1948), pp. 183ff.
11. Cf. Bossert, Gustav, ed., *Quellen zur Geschichte der Weidertäufer I: Herzogtum Wuerttemberg* (M. Heinsius Nachf., 1930), Leipzig. XIII *Quellen und Forschungen zur Reformationsgeschichte:* 1-2, 3-5. Hereafter, *WtQ1930*.
12. Usher, Roland G., *The Presbyterian Movement in the Reign of Queen Elizabeth* (Royal Historical Society, 1905), London, p. xviii.
13. Frere, W. H., and Douglas, C. E., ed., *Puritan Manifestoes . . .* (S. P. C. K., 1907), London, p. 6.
14. *Ecumenical Press Service* (7/11/47) 27:5-6.
15. Herman, Stewart W., "Church and State in Sweden," LXX *The Christian Century* (1953) 8:218-20.
16. *Towards the Conversion of England* (The Church Assembly, 1943), London, pp. 40-41.
17. Brandt, Otto H., *Thomas Muentzer: Sein Leben und seine Schriften* (Eugen Diedrichs Verlag, 1933), Jena, p. 3.
18. Strobel, Georg Theodor, *Leben, Schriften und Lehren Thomas Muenzers* (Monath and Kussler, 1795), Nuernberg and Altdorf, p. 35, quoted.
19. Quoted in Bloch, Ernst, *Thomas Muenzer als Theologe der Revolution* (Kurt Wolff Verlag, 1921), Muenchen, p. 60.
20. Boehmer, Heinrich, *Studien zu Thomas Muentzer* (Alex. Edelmann, 1922), Leipzig, p. 17.
21. Bouterwek, K. W., "Zur Wiedertaeufer-Literatur," I *Zeitschrift des Bergischen Geschichtsvereins* (1864) 3:280-344, 304.
22. *Ibid.*, quoted p. 338.
23. Robertson, D. B., *The Religious Foundations of Leveller Democracy* (King's Crown Press, 1951), N. Y., pp. 111f.
24. Woodhouse, A. S. P., ed., *Puritanism and Liberty* (J. M. Dent and Sons, Ltd., 1938), London, p. 244.

25. Stroup, Herbert Hewitt, *The Jehovah's Witnesses* (Columbia University Press, 1945), N. Y., pp. 44, 84-85.
26. *Ibid.*, p. 165.
27. Müntzer started with individual mysticism (Tauler and Suso) and ended up with the sword in hand in the last days; Joris began where Müntzer arrived and worked back to a point not far from where he began. Cf. Bainton, Roland H., *David Joris: Wiedertaeufer und Kaempfer fuer Toleranz im 16 Jahrhundert* (M. Heinsius Nachf., 1937), Leipzig, p. 10. Bossert, Gustav, "Augustin Bader von Augsburg, der Prophet und Koenig, und seine Genossen, nach den Prozessakten von 1530," X *Archiv fuer Reformationsgeschichte: Texte and Untersuchungen* (1912/13) 117-65, 209-41, 297-349.
28. Bainton, Roland H., "The Immoralities of the Patriarchs According to the Exegesis of the Late Middle Ages and of the Reformation," 23 *Harvard Theological Review* (1930), pp. 39-49, 44.
29. Hegler, A., *Geist und Schrift bei Sebastian Franck* (J. C. B. Mohr, 1892), Freiburg i. Br. Troeltsch, Ernst, *The Social Teachings of the Christian Churches* (Macmillan Co., 1931), N. Y., II, 741ff.
30. Joh. Buenderlin, quoted p. 155 in Nicoladoni, Alexander, *Johannes Buenderlin von Linz und die oberoesterreichischen Taeufergemeinden in den Jahren 1525-1531* (R. Gaertners Verlag, 1893), Berlin.
31. Keller, Ludwig, *Ein Apostel der Wiedertaeufer* (S. Hirzel, 1882), Leipzig, pp. 68-72.
32. Glawe, Walther, *Sebastian Francks Unkirchliches Christentum* (Doerffling & Franke, 1912), Leipzig, p. 47.
33. French, James Leslie, ed., *The Correspondence of Caspar Schwenckfeld of Ossig and the Landgrave Philip of Hesse, 1535-1561* (Breitkopf & Haertel, 1908), Leipzig, p. 65.
34. Wach, Joachim, "Caspar Schwenckfeld, a Pupil and a Teacher in the School of Christ," XXVI *The Journal of Religion* (1946) 1:1-29, 5.
35. Lowrie, Walter, *Kierkegaard* (Oxford University Press, 1938), London, p. 313.
36. Booth, Edwin P., *The Greater Church of the Future* (Beacon Press, 1951), Boston, p. x.
37. *Ibid.*, pp. 10-11, 21.
38. "A Map of Theology Today," Supplement to No. 232 *The Christian News-Letter* (4/18/45). For criticism of the ecumenical movement's "exclusiveness," and the pious hope of a World Parliament of Religions, see Ross, Floyd H., *Addressed to Christians: Isolationism vs. World Community* (Harper & Bros., 1950), N. Y., pp. 12, 14.
39. Romans 8:18f, as translated by Phillips, J. B., *Letters to Young Churches* (Macmillan Co., 1952), N. Y., p. 18.
40. Hubmaier: "eusserlich gmainschafften vnd nit imaginarie." It is clear that Hubmaier is to be reckoned as an Anabaptist, since much of his order at Waldshut was based on believers' baptism and church discipline. But when he was no longer working in Roman Catholic territory as pastor of a Protestant congregation he abandoned much of the central teaching of the movement (Nikolsburg). Quotation is from Sachsse, Carl, *D. Balthasar Hubmaier als Theologie* (Trowitsch & Sohn, 1914), Berlin, p. 187.

41. Yoder, Edward, ed., *Epistolae Grebelianae, 1517-1525;* MSS in the Mennonite Historical Library, Goshen, Indiana, pp. 195-96. Hans Hut, in *Vom Geheimnus der Tauf,* wrote in his vivid style in defense of the radicals and repudiation of the Reformers: "Whoever, my dearest brethren in the Lord, would learn rightly the judgment of God and the sign of the holy writ in truth, should turn not to the noise of the hired preachers, but look to the poor, the despised of the world, those called enthusiasts and devils according to the model of Christ and the apostles. Listen to them. For no one can reach the Truth unless he follows the footsteps of Christ and his elect in the valley of suffering, or at least has in part decided to follow them according to the will of God in the justification of the Cross of Christ. For no one may learn the secret of divine wisdom in the dens and murderous alleys of all knavery as declared in Wittenberg or Paris." Mueller, Lydia, *Glaubenszeugnisse oberdeutscher Taufgesinnter,* I (M. Heinsius Nachf., 1938), Leipzig. XX *Quellen und Forschungen zur Reformationsgeschichte:* 14. Hereafter, *WtQ1938.*
42. Hans Schlaffer, in *WtQ1938,* p. 92.
43. As Champlin Burrage long ago understood, in spite of the imperfect sources upon which he built his interpretation; cf. *The Church Covenant Idea* (American Baptist Publication Society, 1904), Phila., Chap. I.
44. Krahn, Cornelius, *Der Gemeindebegriff des Menno Simons im Rahmen seines Lebens und seiner Theologie* (Heinrich Schneider, 1936), Karlsruhe, pp. 6-7.
45. *WtQ1938,* pp. 204, 147.
46. *Ibid.,* p. 61.
47. Schornbaum, Karl, ed., *Quellen zur Geschichte der Wiedertäufer, II: Markgraftum Brandenburg* (M. Heinsius Nachf., 1934), Leipzig. XVI *Quellen und Forschungen zur Reformationsgeschichte:* 28. Hereafter, *WtQ1934.*
48. From John Smyth's Confession of Faith, c. 1620; Jordan, W. K., *The Development of Religious Toleration in England (1603-1640)* (Harvard University Press, 1936), Cambridge, pp. 269-70.
49. Burrage, Champlin, *The Early English Dissenters . . .* (University Press, 1912), Cambridge, England, quoting John Smyth, II, 172f.
50. Quoted in Atkins, Gaius Glenn, "An Adventure in Liberty," *The Missionary Herald* (January, 1947), p. 8. On the meaning of the Salem Covenant, see Stoughton excerpt in Miller, Perry, and Johnson, Thomas H., *The Puritans* (American Book Company, 1938), N. Y., pp. 243-46.
51. Robinson, John, *A Justification of Separation from the Church of England* (1610), p. 221.

CHAPTER III. *The Free Churches and Political Self-Government*

1. Jenkins, Daniel T., *Church Meeting and Democracy* (Independent Press, Ltd., 1944), London, p. 10.
2. Lindsay, A. D., *The Essentials of Democracy* (University of Pennsylvania Press, 1929), Phila., pp. 19, 37.

3. Cf. Talmon, J. L., *The Origins of Totalitarian Democracy* (Secker & Warburg, 1952), London.
4. Lindsay, A. D., *op., cit.,* p. 40.
5. "Many young men, who have been assured that only the individual counts among us, have died upon foreign battlefields." Niebuhr, Reinhold, *The Irony of American History* (Charles Scribner's Sons, 1952), N. Y., p. 10.
6. *The Universities in Transformation* (Sheldon Press, 1940), London, p. 6.
7. *Bulletin der Presse- und Informationsamtes der Bundesregierung* (Bonn: 1/13/54), p. 49. In Ibrahimov's *The Soviet Union, Land of True Freedom of Conscience* (1949) the statement appears: "The Soviet State, which has carried into effect the principle of the separation of Church and State, regards the Church as a private society with limited functions concerned solely with performing acts of worship. It is only within these functions that the Church is considered as an organized body. All other undertakings, particularly in the social and political field, are plainly unsuited to the Church as a whole, and must therefore not be allowed." Quoted in *The Free Churches and the State* (Free Church Federal Council, 1953), London, p. 10.
8. Cf. Penn's *The Great Case of Liberty of Conscience once more briefly debated, etc.* (1670).
9. On the actual situation in Great Britain, see *The Free Churches and the State,* pp. 24-25.
10. Cf. Fagley, Richard M., *Religious Liberty: Bulwark of Freedom* (NCCC, 1952), N. Y., p. 6. *Universal Declaration of Human Rights* (U. S. Government Printing Office, 1949), Washington, D. C., Department of State Publication 3381.
11. On the direct contribution to the founding of the Republic, through the political activity of clergymen in the Committees of Correspondence, and the importance of the First Great Awakening in building intercolonial communications, see Baldwin, Alice M., *The New England Clergy and the American Revolution* (Duke University Press, 1928), Durham, N. C., p. 138.
12. Cf. Schaff, Philip, "Church and State in the United States," II *Papers of the American Historical Association* (1889), pp. 13-15.
13. *Mysticism and Democracy in the English Commonwealth* (Harvard University Press, 1932), Cambridge, pp. 32-33.
14. This useful phrase gained currency following Roland H. Bainton's article, "The Left Wing of the Reformation," XXI *The Journal of Religion* (1941) 2:124-34.
15. Quoted in May, T. E., *The Constitutional History of England* (W. J. Widdleton, Publ., 1866), N. Y., II, 315.
16. *Die Staatsrechtlichen Verhaeltnisse der Deutschen Katholiken . . .* (Verlag von Julius Groos, 1845), Heidelberg, p. 13.
17. Chafee, Zechariah, Jr., *Freedom of Speech* (Harcourt, Brace & Co., 1920), N. Y., p. 5.
18. On this history cf. Hunt, Gaillard, "James Madison and Religious Liberty," I *Annual Report of the American Historical Association* (1901), pp. 427-28.

19. Quoted in Farrand, Max, *The Fathers of the Constitution* (Yale University Press, 1921), New Haven, p. 152.
20. Cf. Roper, Charles Lee, "Why North Carolina at First Refused to Ratify the Federal Constitution," I *Annual Report of the American Historical Association* (1905), pp. 99-107.
21. Quoted in Dodd, W. F., "The First State Constitutional Conventions, 1776-1783," II *American Political Science Review* (1908), pp. 545-46.
22. Cf. a statement by the author, "A Serious Threat to Religious Liberty," CXXVI *Zions Herald* (1948) 1:2; XIII *The Calvin Forum* (1948) 7: 146-47.
23. "If any member is so far fallen as to be separated from God, consequently rebuked by and expelled from the church he must also, according to the doctrine of Christ and His apostles, be shunned and avoided by all members of the church so that we may not become defiled by intercourse with him and partakers of his sins, but that he be made ashamed, affected in his mind, convinced in his conscience and thereby induced to mend his ways" (Dordrecht Confession, 1632). Cf. *RNS: Domestic* (11/7/47). See article in Bender, Harold S., *et al., The Mennonite Encyclopedia* (Scottdale, Penna.: The Mennonite Pub. House, 1956), II, 92-93.
24. LXVIII *The Christian Century* (1951) 11:324. Recently Colorado's Supreme Court has ruled that civil courts have no authority to pass on spiritual, doctrinal, or ecclesiastical matters, and has advised that churches should not have recourse to civil suit. LXXII *The Christian Century* (1955) 39:1109-10.
25. *Render Unto the People* (Abingdon Press, 1947), Nashville, pp. 19-21.
26. This discussion was prepared without the benefit of Merrimon Cuninggim's excellent work, *Freedom's Holy Light* (Harper & Bros., 1955), N. Y.
27. *An Essay Towards Promoting all Necessary and Useful Knowledge* . . . (E. Holt for Robert Clavel, 1697), London, Preface.
28. Cf. an excellent article of that title by Elizabeth Carmen Payne, in LXVIII *The Christian Century* (1951) 4:106-08.
29. (University of Chicago Press, 1945), Chicago, p. 23.
30. President Pusey of Harvard University proposed a corrective procedure to the Public Education Association in October, 1954: "the full use of graduates of liberal arts colleges in the classrooms of the public schools." The New York *Herald Tribune* (10/21/54), p. 13.
31. Smith, Mortimer, "Who Criticizes Public Schools," LXVIII *The Christian Century* (1951) 25:736-38, 738.
32. Dibelius, Otto, *Grenzen des Staates* (Furche-Verlag, 1949), Goettingen, p. 95.
33. Fey, Harold B., "Should Parochial Schools be Taxed?" LXVIII *The Christian Century* (1951) 32:914-16, 916.
34. "Federal Aid to Religious Schools," 62 *School and Society* (1945), pp. 363-65.
35. "Voluntaryism" is the system, "voluntarism" the spirit behind it. Neither is necessarily theological, i.e., synergistic. On the importance of the revivals to the grounding of the principle of voluntaryism in American

church life, and to liberty in the political sphere, see Baird, Robert, *Religion in America* (Harper & Bros., 1844), N. Y., pp. 129f.

36. *Documentary History of the Struggle for Religious Liberty in Virginia* (J. P. Bell Co., 1900), Lynchburg, Va., p. 9.
37. *The Story of the Durham Miners (1662-1921)* (Labour Publ. Co., Ltd., 1921), London, p. 145.
38. "An Exhortation and Caution to Friends Concerning buying and keeping Negroes," in XIII *The Pennsylvania Magazine of History and Biography* (1889), pp. 265-70.
39. Quoted in Russell, Elbert, *A History of Quakerism* (Macmillan Co., 1942), N. Y., p. 248.
40. Zimmermann, Carl E., *Family and Civilization* (Harper & Bros., 1947), N. Y., p. 806.
41. Duvall, Evelyn Millis, *Building Your Marriage;* Public Affairs Pamphlet No. 113, no place, no date.
42. Hershberger, Guy Franklin, *War, Peace, and Nonresistance* (Herald Press, 1944), Scottdale, Penna., pp. 49, 274.
43. In his newly awakened eschatological expectation, based on the ecumenical concern for the understanding and reconciliation of the different Christian denominations in North America, and on the missionary work which has been developing so well; cf. Benz, Ernst, "Pietist and Puritan Sources of Early Protestant World Missions (Cotton Mather and A. H. Francke)," XX *Church History* (1951) 2:28-55, 33.

CHAPTER IV. *The Free Church vs. The "American Religion"*

1. Wach, Joachim, *Sociology of Religion* (University of Chicago Press, 1944), Chicago, p. 148. As in the Early Church, so with the Free Churchmen, "Christianity was not an opinion nor a sentiment but a highly disciplined community able to dictate both the terms of admission and the conditions of remaining within its circle." Foakes-Jackson, F. J., *The Rise of Gentile Christianity* (Hodder & Stoughton, Ltd., 1927), London, p. 220.
2. See Trueblood, Elton, "The Order of the Yoke," LXVIII *The Christian Century* (1951) 49:1404-06, for a contemporary statement of an old Free Church concern.
3. Wach, Joachim, *op. cit.*, p. 110.
4. Nash, Arnold, "The End of the Protestant Era," LXIII *The Christian Century* (1946) 44:1306-08, 1307. "The End of the *Territorial* Church" would have been a better title: there were, and are, Free Churches.
5. Keller, Adolphe, *Church and State on the European Continent* (Willett, Clark & Co., n.d.), Chicago and N. Y., p. 44.
6. Wieman, Henry N. and Regina W., *Normative Psychology of Religion* (Thomas Y. Crowell Co., 1935), N. Y., p. 29.
9. Booth, Edwin P., *The Greater Church of the Future* (Beacon Press, 1951), Boston, pp. 34-35. Almost as appalling as the theological deficiency displayed is the lack of information as to what scientists themselves are saying and thinking. "It is one of the engaging ironies of modern thought that the scientific method, which it was once fondly hoped would banish mystery from the world, leaves it every day

more inexplicable." Becker, Carl L., *The Heavenly City of the Eighteenth-Century Philosophers* (Yale University Press, 1932), New Haven, p. 24. For a brilliant presentation of the predicament of the nuclear scientists, see Michael Amrine's "The Scientist as Hamlet," XXXV *The Saturday Review of Literature* (1952) 40:9ff. Of another age where similar ideas worked out their natural conclusion in revolution and despotism it has been written: "But that 'enlightened reason' which celebrated its classical triumphs in the eighteenth century knew comparatively little; its sympathies were few, its intelligence limited, and it had lost all inner contact with the mysteries of the historical life. This blindness of the 'enlightened' reason was the inner penalty it paid for its self-assertiveness and for the egoism with which it enslaves both human and the superhuman." Berdyaev, Nicolas, *The Meaning of History* (Charles Scribner's Sons, 1936), N. Y., p. 7.

8. Cf. Buchheim, Hans, *Glaubenskrise im Dritten Reich* (Deutsche Verlagsanstalt, 1935), Stuttgart, p. 17. "Die Behauptung der Nationalsozialisten, es habe in Deutschland seit langer Zeit nicht so viel 'Glaubigkeit' gegeben, wie etwa im Jahre 1933 oder in der Zeit des Krieges, ist nicht falsch; jedoch war es ein in jeder Beziehung entarteter Glaube, ein falscher Glaube nach Inhalt, Intention und Weise."
9. Cf. "The Anabaptist Theology of Missions," XXI *The Mennonite Quarterly Review* (1947) 1:5-17.
10. Loew, Cornelius, "The Sectarianism of John Wesley's Churchmanship," MSS at Lane Hall, Ann Arbor, 1948. Wesley's emphasis upon organizational integrity and a high doctrine of the Church has led many historians to misunderstand his role as a Free Churchman.
11. Quoted in Rigg, James H., *The Churchmanship of John Wesley* (Wesleyan-Methodist Book-Room, 1886), London, p. 25.
12. Hobhouse, W., *The Church and the World in Idea and in History* (Macmillan & Co., Ltd., 1910), London, p. 124.
13. Edited by Nehemiah Curnock (Epworth Press, 1938), London.
14. Against the "American religion," with its banalities and cosmic spiritual voids, see a superb critical review of Hall and Holisher, *Protestant Panorama: The Story of the Faith that made America Free* (New York, 1951) by Robert Clemmer in XXI *Church History* (1952) 2: 170-71. Also Eckhardt, A. Roy, "The New Look in American Piety," LXXI *The Christian Century* (1954) 46:1395-97; Miller, William Lee, "Piety Along the Potomac," XI *The Reporter* (1954) 3:25-28.
15. Dr. W. A. Visser 't Hooft. Even so is it with pastoral prayer. "It is liable to wander between informing God and informing the congregation on the state of the world. The purpose of prayer is to pray." Richardson, Cyril, "Some Thoughts on the Reform of Protestant Worship," XV *Religion in Life* (1946) 4:541f. "Firstly, true Christian prayer always takes place within the Church and is always on behalf of the Church. . . . True prayer is, therefore, pre-eminently Biblical prayer, the prayer of those whose home is the world of the Bible and who daily hear God speaking to them from it." Daniel Jenkins in "Concerning Prayer," Supplement No. 106 to *The Christian News-Letter* (1942).

16. "Deep in the Heart of Texas . . ." in LXIX *The Christian Century* (1952) 46:1312-18; quotation from p. 1315.
17. *Bericht ueber die Verhandlungen des 5. Evangelischen Sozialkongresses* . . . (Verlag von Rehtwitsch & Langewort, 1894), Berlin, pp. 136-173. Contrast the report on the intermediate years in Trotsky, Leon, *Stalin* (Harper & Bros., 1941), N. Y. and London, 2d edition, p. xiii: "This throwback to the most cruel Machiavellianism seems incomprehensible to one who until yesterday abided in the comforting confidence that human history moves along a rising line of material and cultural progress. . . . All of us, I think, can say now: No epoch of the past was so cruel, so ruthless, so cynical as our epoch. Politically, morality has not improved at all by comparison with the standards of the Renaissance and with even more distant epochs." Trotsky was killed by an ice pick, skillfully driven into the back of his head by a Stalinist agent.
18. *The Predicament of Modern Man* (Harper & Bros., 1944), N. Y. and London, p. 3.
19. *This I Believe* (Simon and Schuster, 1952), N. Y., *passim.*
20. "What is the Christian Hope?" in LXIX *The Christian Century* (1952) 15:426-29, 528. For a flippant attack, and Henry P. Van Dusen's protest, cf. LXIX *The Christian Century* (1952) 15:424-25 and LXIX *The Christian Century* (1952) 19:563.
21. LXIX *The Christian Century* (1952) 4:103.
22. Niebuhr, H. Richard, *The Kingdom of God in America* (Willett, Clark & Co., 1937), Chicago, p. 193.
23. LXIX *The Christian Century* (1952) 37:1032.
24. *The Social Teaching of the Christian Churches* (Macmillan Co., 1931), N. Y., I, 445.
25. Schleiermacher, F. D. E., *Soliloquies* (Open Court Publ. Co., 1926), Chicago, pp. 51-52.
26. Quoted in Ergang, Robert Reinhold, *Herder and the Foundations of German Nationalism* (Columbia University dissertation, 1931), N. Y., p. 250. The study by Koppel S. Pinson, *Pietism as a Factor in the Rise of German Nationalism* (Columbia University dissertation, 1934), N. Y., is a particularly brilliant interpretation of the way in which the German nation became a "fellowship group."
27. Cf. my discussion in "The Protestant Churches and Totalitarianism (Germany, 1933-1945)," in Friedrich, Carl J., ed., *Totalitarianism* (Harvard University Press, 1954), Cambridge, pp. 108-19.
28. Hayes Beall in LXII *The Christian Century* (1945) 29:840.
29. *RNS:Domestic* (3/10/47).
30. *RNS:Domestic* (3/11/47).
31. *Op. cit.*, pp. ix-x.
32. "What I Found in Latin America," LXII *The Christian Century* (1945) 30:860.
33. "The Laws of Ecclesiastical Polity," in Fosdick, Harry Emerson, ed., *Great Voices of the Reformation* (Random House, 1952), N. Y., pp. 348-49.
34. Cf. Dexter, Henry Martyn, *The True Story of John Smyth the Se-Baptist* (Lee & Shepard, 1881), Boston, p. 30.

35. Burrage, Champlin, *The Early English Dissenters . . .* (University Press, 1912), Cambridge, quoted, II, 185.
36. The Communion of Saints is as real to the Free Churches as to the establishments. There is in their genius no break from a continuing Covenant. They forswear the "rude political arbitrament of a living majority, when the real spiritual majority are the dead." Peter Taylor Forsyth, quoted by Jenkins, D. T., *Church Meeting and Democracy* (Independent Press, Ltd., 1944), London, p. 27. On the continuing tradition generally, cf. "The Anabaptists and Christian Tradition," IV *The Journal of Religious Thought* (1947) 2:167-81.

CHAPTER V. *The Free Church vs. Totalitarianism*

1. *Faith, Freedom, and the Future* (Hodder & Stoughton, n.d.), N. Y. and London, pp. 61, 200.
2. Niemoeller, Martin, *First Commandment* (Wm. Hodge & Co., Ltd., 1937), London, p. 238.
3. Feder, Gottfried, *Das Programm der N.S.D.A.P. und seine weltanschaulichen Grundgedanken* (Verlag Frz. Eher Nachf., 1933), Muenchen. *Nationalsozialistiche Bibliothek,* Heft 1, p. 22. Cf. discussion of this and related points in "Pastoral Care Under Totalitarianism," XIII *Christianity and Crisis* (1953) 6:42-46.
4. (Willett, Clark & Co., n.d.), Chicago and N. Y., p. 44.
5. Visser 't Hooft, W. A., *"None Other Gods"* (Harper & Bros., 1937), N. Y. and London, p. 70.
6. "Barth to Bereczky," LXIX *The Christian Century* (1952) 31:876-77.
7. *The Great Society* (Macmillan Co., 1914), N. Y. On the American development today see Riesman, David, *et al., The Lonely Crowd* (Doubleday Anchor Books, 1954), Garden City, N. Y. On mobs in wartime: "The facts of history are that the wars waged by the old dynasties and the old aristocracies were wars waged with moderation and restraint, while the wars waged in the name of a 'people's' revolution and in an age in which the main appeal is made to the masses have been less limited, more destructive, and totalitarian." Jones, Aubrey, *The Pendulum of Politics* (Faber & Faber, Ltd., 1946), London, p. 53.
8. Henry Knox Sherrill, quoted in Thelen, Mary Frances, *Man as Sinner: in Contemporary American Realistic Theology* (King's Crown Press, 1946), Morningside Heights, N. Y., p. 127, footnote.
9. Ferre, Nels F. S., "The Holy Spirit and the Individual," III *The Asbury Seminarian* (1948) 3:96-102, 101.
10. Horsch, John, *The Hutterian Brethren, 1528-1931* (Mennonite Historical Society, 1931), Goshen, Indiana, p. 134, footnote 128.
11. Thelen, Mary Frances, *op. cit.,* p. 156.
12. *The Myth of the State* (Yale University Press, 1946), New Haven, p. 109.
13. *Toward Christian Democracy* (Geo. Allen & Unwin, Ltd., 1945), London, p. 55.
14. Andre Gide, in Crossman, Richard, ed., *The God That Failed* (Harper & Bros., 1949), N. Y., pp. 188, 183.
15. (Furche-Verlag, 1949), Goettingen. Summary of material in Section 11, pp. 82ff.

16. Quoted in Viereck, Peter, *Conservatism Revisited* (Charles Scribner's Sons, 1950), N. Y. and London, pp. 84-85.
17. *European Issues,* No. 5 (10/11/54), pp. 1-2 (Casa Postale 16, Geneva 17, Switzerland).
18. "Functional Democracy in Human Relations," in Cook, Lloyd Allen, ed., *Toward Better Human Relations* (Wayne University Press, 1952), Detroit, pp. 28-29.
19. The king was considered also subject to the terms of his oath and Covenant; cf. Rutherford, Samuel, *Lex, Rex* (John Field, 1644), London, p. 406.
20. Cf. my article on "The Inadequacy of Modern Pacifism," in *Christianity and Society* (1946) 2:18-23.
21. On the effect of persecution in bringing an emphasis on the "inner" among the spiritualizers of the time, see Bainton, Roland H., *David Joris: Wiedertaeufer und Kaempfer fuer Toleranz im 16. Jahrhundert* (M. Heinsius Nachf., 1937), Leipzig, p. 13.
22. Among others, Zieglschmid, A. J. F., ed., *Die aelteste Chronik der Hutterischen Brueder* (Cayuga Press, Inc., 1943), Ithaca, N. Y., p. 309.
23. *WtQ1938,* p. 97.
24. *Ibid.,* p. 186.
25. *Ibid.,* p. 199.
26. Cf. Trueblood, D. Elton, "The Quaker Way," 166 *The Atlantic Monthly* (1940) 6:740-46; Yarrow, Clarence H., "Should the Pacifists Expect Success?" 102 *Friends Intelligencer* (1945) 35:555-56.
27. Hartill, Percy, ed., *Into the Way of Peace* (Fellowship Publications, 1943), N. Y., Chap. I.
28. (Harper Bros., 1948), N. Y.
29. Reinhold Niebuhr in LXVIII *The Christian Century* (1951) 25:743.
30. LXIX *The Christian Century* (1952) 12:332.
31. "Maertyrertheologie und Taeuferbewegung," LII *Zeitschrift fuer Kirchengeschichte* (1933), pp. 545-98, 566.
32. Private report in the hands of the author.
33. *RNS:Domestic* (12/12/52).
34. Quoted in "The Protestant Church in Germany," VII *The World Today* (1951) 10:439-49, 445, by "C.C.W." On the relation of generations, cf. Fisher, Louis, in Crossman, Richard, ed., *op. cit.,* p. 228: "In one's absorption with an ideal, it is possible to imagine that one generation can be sacrificed for the sake of its descendants. But sacrificing people may become a habit unto the second and third generation. I thought, in my Soviet phase, that I was serving humanity. But it is only since then that I have really discovered the human being."
35. Cf. Kirckheimer, Otto, "In Quest of Sovereignty," VI *The Journal of Politics* (1944) 2:139-72.
36. Cf. discussion by the author, "Thoughts About the Future of Christianity and Judaism: A Christian View of Reconstructionism," XIII *The Reconstructionist* (1947) 4:10-16, 5:16-22. Mordecai M. Kaplan shows the acceptance of status as a culture religion for Judaism, in "The Chosen People Idea as Anachronism," XI *The Reconstructionist* (1946) 17:13-20: "the traditional formula concerning Israel's divine election is objectionable. Rationally it has no place in a universe of

discourse from which belief in the supernatural revelation of religious truth is excluded." He was answering an excellent article by Bernard J. Bamberger, "Are the Jews a Chosen People?" XI *The Reconstructionist* (1945) 16:16-19, which explained the balance of election and universalism which is the Biblical revelation, and concluded: "If few Jews today desire proselytes, it is because their missionary zeal, so long suppressed, has become atrophied." On the need for positive discipline in the Jewish communities, see Judah Goldin's "Living in a Religious Climate," XII *The Reconstructionist* (1947) 18:10-17. The ghetto of the Jews was a function of Christendom, in its old coercive pattern; like the territorial establishments, the Jews also lost their universalism.

37. Lenin, V. I., *What is to Be Done?* (International Publishers, 1929), N. Y., p. 131. "The rise of communism in our world is comparable to the rise of Islam and its challenge of Christian civilization in the high Middle Ages. Some of the measures we take against it are informed by the same lack of realism which characterized the Crusades. The Islamic power finally waned. It was destroyed not so much by its foes as by it own inner corruptions. The Sultan of Turkey found it ultimately impossible to support the double role of political head of a nation and the spiritual head of the Islamic world. Stalin has this same double role in the world of communist religion. He or his successors will finally be convicted of insinuating the power impulse of a Russian state into the Messianic illusions of an ostensibly world-wide political religion. If we fully understand the deep springs which feed the illusions of this religion, the nature of the social resentments which nourish them and the realities of life which must ultimately refute them, we might acquire the necessary patience to wait out the long run of history while we take such measures as are necessary to combat the more immediate perils." Niebuhr, Reinhold, *The Irony of American History* (Charles Scribner's Sons, 1952), N.Y., pp. 128-29.
38. "Spiritual Problems of Post-War Reconstruction," II *Christianity and Crisis* (1942) 14:2-6, 5.
39. Brunner, Emil, *The Church and the Oxford Group* (Hodder & Stoughton, 1937), London, pp. 60-61.

CHAPTER VI. *The Free Church and its Discipline*

1. *The Church and the Political Problem of Our Day* (Charles Scribner's Sons, 1939), N. Y., pp. 82-83.
2. Ludlow, Wilma, "Inasmuch as We Did It Not," LVI *The Christian Century* (1939) 44:1336-37.
3. *The Missionary Message in Relation to Non-Christian Religions* (Fleming H. Revell Co., 1910), N. Y., p. 244.
4. Supplement No. 172 to *The Christian News-Letter* (1943). Is there any relation here with the report that the "Bishop of Winchester has recently confessed that the book which he uses as his text-book for Confirmation is *Scouting for Boys*"? Baden-Powell, Robert, *Scoutmastership* (G. P. Putnam's Sons, 1928), N. Y. and London, Intr.
5. V *Opinion News*, University of Denver (12/25/45), p. 13.
6. Latourette, Kenneth S., *A History of the Expansion of Christianity* (Harper & Bros., 1937-45), N. Y. and London, IV, 177.

7. *Information Bulletin of the Federal Council of Churches* (December, 1945).
8. *Church and State in the United States* (G. P. Putnam's Sons, 1888), N. Y. and London, p. 81.
9. Hayward, Percy R., and Burkhart, Roy A., *Young People's Method in the Church* (Abingdon Press, 1933), N. Y., p. 221.
10. *RNS:Domestic* (3/20/45).
11. LXIV *The Christian Century* (1947) 49:1500.
12. LXVI *The Christian Century* (1949) 52:1545.
13. *RNS:Foreign* (12/23/52).
14. XXXVII *The Modern Churchman* (1947) 1:7-8.
15. Bouma, Clarence, "Three Reformed Pillars," XII *The Calvin Forum* (1947) 10:205.
16. *Resolving Social Conflicts* (Harper & Bros., 1948), N. Y., pp. 66-67.
17. Newcomb, Theodore M., *Personality and Social Change: Attitude Formation in a Student Community* (Dryden Press, 1943), N. Y.
18. Cf. my article on the Restitution of the True Church, XXVI *The Mennonite Quarterly Review* (1950) 1:33-52.
19. Cf. Hughes, Edwin Holt, "Our Mistaken Legislation on Amusements," 106 *The Methodist Review* (1923), pp. 719-29.
20. Schleitheim Confession (1527); Boehmer, Heinrich, ed., "Urkunden zur Geschichte des Bauernkrieges und der Wiedertaeufer," 50/51 *Kleine Texte fuer Theologische und Philologische Vorlesungen und Uebungen* (1910), pp. 25f.
21. *WtQ1938*, p. 27.
22. *WtQ1934*, pp. 70-71.
23. J. H. Oldham, reviewing Leslie Paul's *The Annihilation of Man;* in No. 218 *The Christian News-Letter.*
24. Lehmann, Paul, in Hutchinson, John A., ed., *Christian Faith and Social Action* (Charles Scribner's Sons, 1953), N. Y. and London, pp. 102f.
25. Deets, Lee Emerson, *The Hutterites: A Study in Social Cohesion* (publ. by author, 1939), Gettysburg, Penna., p. 1.
26. "The Class meeting is a test of membership. The Holy Table cannot be approached, as a matter of course, by any except those 'who meet in class.' Every holder of office of any kind must be found using this prudential regulation." Murray, Robert H., *Group Movements Throughout the Ages* (Hodder & Stoughton, Ltd., 1935), London, p. 264.
27. Cf. James H. Nichols in LXVIII *The Christian Century* (1951) 28:821-22.
28. *Op. cit.*, p. 35.
29. Bainton, Roland H., *David Joris: Wiedertaeufer und Kaempfer fuer Toleranz im 16. Jahrhundert* (M. Heinsius Nachf., 1937), Leipzig, quoted on p. 44.
30. Cf. the first article in Paracelsus' *De septem punctis idolatriae Christianae;* Peuckert, Will-Erich, *Pansophie* (W. Kohlhammer Verlag, 1936), Stuttgart, p. 261.
31. In Virginia, 1663; the work of Fox and Edmundson to undo the damage of his spiritualizing led to the setting up of meetings for discipline among the Societies; Weeks, Stephen B., *Southern Quakers and Slavery* (Johns Hopkins University Press, 1896), Baltimore, pp. 27-28.

32. *Acta des gespraechs zwueschenn predicanntenn Vnnd Tauffbruederenn Erganngen, Inn der Statt Bernn* . . . (MSS in Mennonite Historical Library, Goshen, Indiana, from Volume 80 of *Unnuetzen Papiere* in Staatsarchiv Kantons Bern), p. 30.
33. Friedmann, Robert, *Mennonite Piety Through the Centuries* (Mennonite Historical Society, 1949), Goshen, Indiana, p. 29.
34. Schultz, Selina Gerhard, *Caspar Schwenckfeld von Ossig (1489-1561)* (Board of Publ. of the Schwenckfelder Church, 1946), Norristown, Penna, p. 285.
35. United Press release, October 16, 1954.
36. *WtQ1930,* p. 167.
37. "Die Kirche . . . die lebendige Gemeinde des lebendigen Herrn Jesus Christus;" MSS for Commission I of the World Council of Churches (April, 1947), privately circulated.
38. *The Quakers: A Study in Costume* (Ferris & Leach, 1901), Phila., pp. 17, 63, 228.
39. Fleming, Daniel J., *Ventures in Simpler Living* (International Missionary Council, 1933), N. Y.

CHAPTER VII. *The Free Churches and Ecumenics*

1. *The Christian Approach to the Moslem* (Columbia University Press, 1942), N. Y., p. 66.
2. It is significant, however, that the foreign missionary movement was the first outside religious environmental influence to be taken up in the Mennonite churches; cf. Pannabecker, Samuel Floyd, *The Development of the General Conference of the Mennonite Church of North American in the American Environment* (Yale University Ph.D. MSS, 1944), New Haven, pp. 36, 618.
3. "We are Men and Not God," LXV *The Christian Century* (1948) 43: 1138-40, 1139.
4. Mecklin, John M., *The Story of American Dissent* (Harcourt, Brace & Co., 1934), N. Y., p. 16.
5. *The Missionary Message in Relation to Non-Christian Religions* (Fleming H. Revell Co., 1910), N. Y., p. 251.
6. *The Christian Message in a Non-Christian World* (Harper & Bros., 1938), N. Y. and London, pp. 16-17.
7. See his *The Idea of a Christian Society* (Harcourt, Brace & Co., 1940), N. Y.
8. Hoekendijk, Hans, "Consolation in Despair," XXXVIII *The Student World* (1945) 4:281-85, 281.
9. In "'As the Truth is in Jesus' (Ephes. 4:21)," LXVIII *The Christian Century* (1951) 51:1457-59.
10. Gurian, Waldemar, "Totalitarianism as Political Religion," in Friedrich, Carl J., ed., *Totalitarianism* (Harvard University Press, 1954), Cambridge, pp. 119-29, 122-23. On Communism as a religion of salvation, see also Gollwitzer, Helmut, "Kann ein Christ Communist Sein?" reprint from *Kirche und Mann* (Guetersloh, n.d.), p. 5.
11. Miller, Alexander, *The Christian Significance of Karl Marx* (Macmillan Co., 1947), N. Y., p. 82. At the Leipzig Kirchentag, 1954, Bishop Lilje

preached on Revelation 2, and described the struggle with Satan as a real encounter.

12. Beck, Josef, ed., *Die Geschichts-Buecher der Wiedertäufer in Oesterreich-Ungarn* (Carl Gerold's Sohn, 1883), Vienna, p. 39, footnote 2.
13. *WtQ1930,* p. 1068.
14. Braithwaite, William C., *The Beginnings of Quakerism* (Macmillan & Co., Ltd., 1912), London, p. 337.
15. Hopkins, Charles Howard, *The Rise of the Social Gospel in American Protestantism, 1865-1915* (Yale University Press, 1940), New Haven, pp. 205ff.
16. Quoted in Paton, William, *A Faith for the World* (Edinburgh House Press, 1929), London, p. 113.
17. Leber, Annedore, *et al., Das Gewissen Steht Auf* (Mosaik Verlag, 1954), Berlin and Frankfurt, p. 164.
18. When asked in 1941 what he was praying for Bonhoeffer said: "If you really want to know, I am praying for the defeat of my country, because I believe that is the only way in which my country can pay for all the suffering it has caused in the world." Quoted in Herman, Stewart, *The Rebirth of the German Church* (S. C. M. Press, 1946), London, p. 90.
19. Leiper, Henry Smith, "From Pulpit to Prison," an appendix to Martin Niemoeller's *From U-Boat to Pulpit* (Willett, Clark & Co., 1937), Chicago and New York, p. 205.
20. Visser 't Hooft, W. A., ed., *The Struggle of the Dutch Church* (American Committee for the World Council of Churches, 1945), N. Y., p. 63.
21. *Ibid.,* 16-17.
22. *Auf verlorenem Posten?* (Im Furche-Verlag, 1948), Tübingen, p. 148.
23. Reported in LXIX *The Christian Century* (1952) 16:473-74.
24. *The Social Sources of Denominationalism* (Henry Holt & Co., 1929), N. Y., p. 275.
25. Landis, Benson Y., *Yearbook of American Churches* (NCCC, 1956), N. Y. Complete figures as of 1954.

Index

Index